CONTEMPORARY'S

Breakthroughs

in Writing and Language

CONTEMPORARY'S
Breakthroughs
in Writing and Language

Developing the Writing Process
Joan Maruskin-Mott

CONTEMPORARY
BOOKS

A TRIBUNE NEW MEDIA/EDUCATION COMPANY

Library of Congress Cataloging-in-Publication Data
Maruskin-Mott, Joan.
    Breakthroughs in writing and language/Joan Maruskin-Mott.
        p.   cm.
    ISBN 0-8092-3298-7
    1. English language—Composition and exercises—Study and
teaching.   2. Diaries—Authorship.   I. Title.
LB1576.M3796   1996
372.6'23—dc20
                                                        95-42670
                                                        CIP

Project Editors
Joan Conover
Christine Kelner

Published by Contemporary Books, Inc.
Two Prudential Plaza, Chicago, Illinois 60601-6790
Manufactured in the United States of America
International Standard Book Number: 0-8092-3298-7
10 9 8 7 6 5 4 3 2 1

Published simultaneously in Canada by
Fitzhenry & Whiteside
195 Allstate Parkway
Markham, Ontario L3R 4T8
Canada

Consultants/Field Testers
Sr. Kathleen Bahlinger, C.S.J.
Sr. Lory Schaff, C.S.J.

Director, New Product Development
Noreen Lopez

Editorial Director
Mark Boone

Editorial
Elena Delaney
Maggie McCann
Gretchen Miller

Design and Production Manager
Norma Underwood

Cover Design
Michael Kelly

Production Artist
Thomas D. Scharf

Interior Illustrations
David Will

Cover Images
Image Bank; Stock Imagery

Contents

TO THE INSTRUCTOR

Contemporary's *Breakthroughs in Writing and Language* is designed to help students develop a firm basis in writing and language skills. As the title indicates, both the process of writing and conventions of English are covered. In particular, there are three features to note:

- The "Journal Writing" feature provides students with a variety of ideas for writing in their journals. Its main purpose is to help students start to feel comfortable as writers. In this section *only*, grammar and spelling are not emphasized.
- "Putting Your Skills to Work," a highly structured writing activity, appears following language skills exercises. The writing focuses on the grammar point that was just taught. This feature helps students to understand grammar in the context of their own writing.
- Somewhat less structured than "Putting Your Skills to Work," "Your Turn to Write" gives students a choice of topics and some suggestions about how to approach the topic. "Your Turn to Write" is followed by a checklist of a few of the major grammar and usage points in the chapter. The checklist guides students in editing their own writing.

As you can see, each of these writing activities serves a slightlydifferent function. It may be useful to alert students to the differences between the three activities.

Other features of the book concentrate exclusively on grammar and usage. Each "Language Skills" section covers a different point in conventions of English. A chapter review follows each "Language Skills" section. "Punctuating Perfectly" highlights punctuation issues related to grammar issues in the text.

Research has shown that teaching the process of writing in conjunction with grammar and usage is a highly effective way of helping students to become better writers. *Breakthroughs in Writing and Language* incorporates this combined approach, and we hope that you and your students will benefit from it.

TO THE STUDENT

Congratulations! As you start work in *Breakthroughs in Writing and Language,* you are on your way to becoming a better writer. You'll get plenty of practice in writing, and you'll gain a good understanding of basic grammar and usage.

Before you begin work in this book, take the pre-test. It will help you decide which chapters you need to concentrate on as you work through the book. When you are finished with the book, the post-test will help you evaluate the work you have done.

Although you may find many of the exercises in this book to be useful, remember that the best way to learn writing is to write. Take advantage of writing opportunities in your everyday life. Every time you write a letter, leave a note for a family member, or even make a grocery list, you are practicing your writing skills.

Good luck!

PRE-TEST

This pre-test is a chance for you to test your present writing skills. The pre-test will show you the kinds of things you will be studying in this text and will help you identify the areas you should work on most.

Follow the directions before each section of the pre-test and answer as many of the questions as possible. If you're not certain about an answer, use the answer that first comes to mind. For this test, you don't have to worry about your score. It is only important that you answer to the best of your ability.

Once you have completed the pre-test, check your answers on pages 7–8. Take time to compare all answers. Sometimes just seeing the right answer to a question will help you remember a writing skills rule you haven't used in a long time.

SECTION I

PART 1: COMPLETE SENTENCES AND SUBJECTS

This section will help you find out if you can recognize a complete sentence. It will also tell you if you can find the subject of a sentence.

Directions: Each of the following pairs of sentences contains one complete sentence and one fragment. Circle the letter of the complete sentence in each pair. Then underline the subject of the complete sentence. The first one has been done as an example.

1. **a.** At Dinah's house after the movie.
   (b.) The <u>party</u> starts after the movie.

2. **a.** The role of computers in the plant.
   b. The computers do much of the work.

3. **a.** Roger is going to the office now.
   b. Going to the office this morning.

4. **a.** Sara not on this committee.
   b. Sara will speak at the meeting.

5. **a.** Will Carla go out with her parents tonight?
   b. Going out tonight?

6. **a.** You passed the test easily.
   b. Took the test two weeks ago.

PART 2: NOUNS

This section tests your understanding of several types of nouns: common and proper nouns, singular and plural nouns, and possessive nouns.

Directions: Circle the correct noun form in each of the following sentences.

1. In the spring, the *(school, School)* will have driver education classes.

2. The *(women, womens)* are on their way home.

3. The *(bus's, bus')* tires were flat.

4. The *(boys, boy's)* caught five fish last summer.

5. Tomorrow *(aunt, Aunt)* Judy will pick you up at 3:00.

6. All the *(doctors', doctors's)* offices have gray carpeting.

PART 3: PRONOUNS

This section will help you find out whether you can use pronouns correctly.

Directions: Part of each of the following sentences is underlined. In the blank at the end of the sentence, write the pronoun you could use to replace the underlined part. The first one has been done as an example.

1. Bruno will buy <u>pizza</u>. _____*it*_____

2. <u>Patty</u> will bring the tapes. _____

3. <u>The stereo's</u> speakers are fantastic. _____

4. <u>Steve and I</u> will entertain. _____

5. <u>Ethel's</u> best jokes will be told. _____

6. Those jokes will keep <u>the guests</u> laughing. _____

PART 4: VERBS

The following section will help you find out how much you know about verb tenses, common irregular verbs, and subject-verb agreement.

Directions: Underline the correct form of the verb to complete each of the following sentences.

1. The winner *(will receive, will receives)* $50,000.

2. Yesterday the man *(laughs, laughed)* at the television show.

3. They *(write, writes)* letters to their friends.

4. Mike or Diane *(is, are)* in charge of the meeting.

5. Stacy and Mary Lou *(was, were)* at the pool.

6. Jonah *(did, done)* all he could to finish on time.

7. The contestants on stage *(wave, waves)* to the audience.

8. Next time I *(will walk, walked)* another way.

PART 5: ADJECTIVES AND ADVERBS

In this section, you'll be asked to decide whether an adjective or an adverb will correctly complete the sentence. Adjectives describe nouns, and adverbs describe verbs.

Directions: Underline the correct word to complete each of the following sentences.

1. The *(intelligent, intelligently)* professor wrote a book.

2. After the game, Howard drove *(quick, quickly)* home.

3. Grandma baked *(delicious, deliciously)* bread.

4. Raoul swam *(graceful, gracefully)*.

5. Edward spoke *(loud, loudly)*.

PART 6: SENTENCE COMBINING

This section asks you to recognize ways to form sentences that make sense and are punctuated correctly. The first one is done for you.

Directions: Draw lines to connect the thoughts that can be combined to make complete, logical sentences.

1. Alex ran for the train,   she missed my party.

2. Rosa lost her wallet;   nevertheless, she forgave us.

3. Tim worked very hard,   but he missed it.

4. Alice was angry;   although he hates music.

5. Because Cathy went to Boston,   so he got the promotion.

6. Mark went to the concert   therefore, she had to borrow money.

PART 7: PUNCTUATION

This section will help you learn about your punctuation skills.

Directions: Each of the following sentences needs one punctuation mark. Add the punctuation that makes each sentence correct.

1. I ordered pizza salad, and coffee.

2. What happened to the hot water

3. After the soccer team members won the championship they celebrated for two days.

4. Mr. Spagnola your help is needed.

5. I said "I am ready for anything."

6. Tim cant go dancing because he broke his leg.

7. Edwin has three daughters and I have two sons.

8. Celeste Wesson a policewoman, will talk about self-defense.

SECTION II
WRITING SENTENCES

This section tests your writing ability.

Directions: Answer the following questions about yourself *in complete sentences*. Write as correctly as you can.

1. Tell three things you do when you have free time.

_____

_____

_____

2. Write a sentence about what you like to eat for breakfast.

_____

_____

3. Tell why a person you love is very important to you.

_____

_____

4. Describe yourself in three or four sentences. You could tell how tall you are, how old you are, what size you are, and what color hair and eyes you have.

_____

_____

_____

_____

5. If you could have one wish granted, what would that wish be?

_____

_____

Check your work on pages 7–8.

PRE-TEST ANSWER KEY

Section I
Part 1: Complete Sentences and Subjects
1. b party
2. b computers
3. a Roger
4. b Sara
5. a Carla
6. a You

Part 2: Nouns
1. school — No specific school is named, so it is not a proper noun and should not be capitalized.
2. women — *Women* is a plural noun, so it is not necessary to add an *s*.
3. bus's — Add *'s* to a singular noun to show possession.
4. boys — Add *s* to make most nouns plural.
5. Aunt — *Aunt* is used as part of Aunt Judy's name in this sentence, so it should be capitalized.
6. doctors' — Several doctors have offices with gray carpeting. Add an apostrophe to a plural noun ending in *s* to show possession.

Part 3: Pronouns
1. it — The pronoun is the object of the sentence.
2. She — The pronoun is the subject of the sentence.
3. Its — The pronoun must show possession.
4. We — The pronoun is the subject of the sentence.
5. Her — The pronoun must show possession.
6. them — The pronoun is the object of the sentence.

Part 4: Verbs
1. will receive — The future tense is formed by using *will* with the base verb.
2. laughed — The time clue *Yesterday* tells you to put the verb in the past tense.
3. write — To agree with the pronoun *They*, the verb should not end in *s*.
4. is — Because the two parts of the subject are joined by *or*, the verb agrees with the closest part—*Diane*.
5. were — Because the two parts of the subject are joined by *and*, the verb must agree with a plural subject.
6. did — The verb *done* needs a helping verb. *Did* is the correct past tense.
7. wave — The subject, *contestants*, is plural, so the verb must not end in *s*.
8. will walk — The time clue *Next time* tells you to use the future tense.

Part 5: Adjectives and Adverbs
1. intelligent — An adjective must be used to describe the noun *professor*.
2. quickly — An adverb must be used to describe the verb *drove*.
3. delicious — An adjective must be used to describe the noun *bread*.
4. gracefully — An adverb must be used to describe the verb *swam*.
5. loudly — An adverb must be used to describe the verb *spoke*.

Part 6: Sentence Combining
1. Alex ran for the train, but he missed it.
2. Rosa lost her wallet; therefore, she had to borrow money.
3. Tim worked very hard, so he got the promotion.
4. Alice was angry; nevertheless, she forgave us.
5. Because Cathy went to Boston, she missed my party.
6. Mark went to the concert although he hates music.

Part 7: Punctuation

1. I ordered pizza, salad, and coffee.
2. What happened to the hot water?
3. After the soccer team members won the championship, they celebrated for two days.
4. Mr. Spagnola, your help is needed.
5. I said, "I am ready for anything."
6. Tim can't go dancing because he broke his leg.
7. Edwin has three daughters, and I have two sons.
8. Celeste Wesson, a policewoman, will talk about self-defense.

Section II
Writing Sentences

In this part of the pre-test, you had to write on your own. If you had trouble thinking of things to say or writing correctly, don't worry. This book is designed to help you get used to putting your thoughts on paper. It will also help you learn to write correctly.

You may have had a hard time getting ideas on paper. If so, give special effort to journal writing, which is explained on page 10. This kind of writing will help you "get your juices flowing" as a writer. Try to write frequently in your journal. Write several times a week—every day if you can. There is a journal writing activity at the beginning of each chapter, but don't wait for the beginning of a chapter to come around.

You may feel that you need a lot of help in writing correctly. If so, work especially hard on the activities called "Putting Your Skills to Work." These activities are designed to help you practice rules of good English in your writing.

Finally, keep in mind that the best way to improve your writing is to write a lot. You don't have to write perfectly to communicate. You just have to be willing to keep trying!

Here are some sample answers to the questions that you can compare your answers to. Your answers will be different from these.

1. When I have free time, I jog, watch TV, and read.
2. I like to eat bacon and eggs for breakfast.
3. I love my mother because she brought me into this world.
4. I am nineteen years old. I am a huge person who is over six feet tall. I have dark hair and green eyes.
5. If I could have one wish granted, I would wish for more wishes!

PRE-TEST EVALUATION CHART

Check your answers on pages 7–8. Then come back to this chart. Find the number of each question you missed and circle it in the second column. In addition to reviewing the pages listed below, you may want to work through the first chapter.

	Item Number	Study Pages	Number Correct
Part 1 Complete sentences	1, 2, 3, 4, 5, 6	26–38	_____/6
Part 2 Common and proper nouns	1, 5		
Singular and plural nouns	2, 4	45–55	_____/6
Possessive nouns	3, 6		
Part 3 Subject pronouns	2, 4		
Object pronouns	1, 6	55–65	_____/6
Possessive pronouns	3, 5		
Part 4 Verb tenses	1, 2, 8	70–88	
Subject-verb agreement	3, 4, 5, 6, 7	98–110	_____/8
Part 5 Adjectives and adverbs	1, 2, 3, 4, 5	120–131	_____/5
Part 6 Conjunctions	1, 3		
Connectors	2, 4	143–160	_____/6
Dependent conjunctions	5, 6		
Part 7 Comma in a series	1	131–134	
Types of sentences	2	29–31	
Subordinating conjunctions	3	156–159	
Direct address	4	113–114	
Quotation marks	5	88–90	
Contractions	6	62–65	
Conjunctions	7	146–150	
Phrases that give additional information	8	110–111	_____/8

CHAPTER 1

JOURNAL WRITING
YOUR THOUGHTS ABOUT THE WORLD

If you are like many people, the thought of writing can send chills up your spine or ruin a beautiful day. However, many people have discovered that writing in a journal can be the high point of a beautiful day or even a rotten day.

A journal is a place to write down your thoughts and feelings about your world. In a journal entry, you begin by writing your first thoughts and end when you don't have anything else to say. A journal entry can be a few sentences, a few paragraphs, or a few pages. Your journal is one place where you don't have to worry about spelling, grammar, or punctuation. Your only concern is your thoughts. Many times, one thought will lead to another, and you will change topics several times in one journal entry. Your journal grows as you grow. It is a record of the person you are at the moment you are writing.

You can use your journal to sort through thoughts, write letters, argue with your friends, or write about your dreams and goals. Your journal gives you an opportunity to say all the things you've wanted to say.

Your journal is for your eyes only (unless you want to share it with someone). It shows the best of you and sometimes the worst of you, but it's you! A page from one writer's journal follows. Nothing really special happened to the writer that day, but some things about the day brought special thoughts to her mind.

> *May 17*
>
> *Baseball season started today. I never thought I would be spending day after day at Little League games. In grade school, I was always the last person chosen for a team. Being the neighborhood misfit was not the best time of my life. But it helped me learn to not always expect life to be a bed of roses. I really was a lousy ball player. But I had a chance to improve, thank goodness. I never thought I would be an excellent ball player. But my older brother worked with me and helped me. He's a really great guy. . . .*

(That's all the writer wanted to share. Remember, a journal is private. So the writer doesn't have to tell you more about her brother if she doesn't want to.)

Here are some suggestions for journal writing:
1. Get a special journal notebook.
2. Keep it in a safe place.
3. Keep a pen or pencil with your journal.
4. Set aside a certain time each day for journal writing.

Some people get up fifteen minutes early to write in their journals. Some people write during lunch. (Their thoughts grow, and their bodies shrink.) Some people write before going to bed. It doesn't matter what time you choose. Just pick a time when you can have a few moments of quiet.

Some people write in their journals every day. You don't have to. But if you enjoy journal writing, you will probably find yourself adding to your journal on a regular basis.

While working through this book, you will find suggestions for journal writing at the start of each chapter. These are just suggestions. Feel free to write journal entries on any topic you like.

FREEWRITING

If you want to, you can use freewriting for this journal entry. *Freewriting* means writing down the thoughts going through your mind. Before you start, decide how long you will be writing. (Ten minutes is a good length of time.) Then put your pen or pencil to paper and start. Write down anything that comes into your mind. You don't have to stick with a topic. If you get stuck, write the same word over and over until you think of something else. The important thing is to write without stopping for the full ten minutes (or whatever length of time you choose).

JOURNAL ENTRY

Directions: Take some time now to make your first journal entry. If you don't have a special notebook for your journal yet, use a page from any notebook and add it to your journal later.

If you want to, choose one of the incomplete sentences below to begin your first journal entry. Finish the sentence and then add sentences until you are finished writing or run out of time.

My home is . . . .
I wish I were . . . .
My vacation was . . . .
You shouldn't have . . . .
The weekends are . . . .

If you don't like any of these topics, write on anything that interests you. It's *your* journal.

LANGUAGE SKILLS
PARTS OF SPEECH

Before you really begin studying the information in this book, let's look quickly at five parts of speech: nouns, pronouns, verbs, adjectives, and adverbs. They will be discussed briefly in this chapter and explained in more detail later. They are presented here because you often need to be familiar with parts of speech when studying writing skills.

NOUNS

A *noun* names a person, place, thing, or idea.

Here are a few examples of nouns:

Persons	Places	Things	Ideas
uncle	lake	motorcycle	speed
Mr. Archer	stadium	baseball	excitement
Shelley	Knoxville	sweater	fashion
Aunt Rose	ocean	shells	health
lawyer	courthouse	bail	crime
president	White House	dog	hate

There are three nouns in the sentence below. Find and circle them.

Aunt Rose wanted to ride her motorcycle to the ocean.

You were right if you circled *Aunt Rose* (a person), *motorcycle* (a thing), and *ocean* (a place). Now try another sentence containing two nouns. One of the nouns is an idea.

The lawyer learned that crime doesn't pay.

The nouns in that sentence are *lawyer* and *crime*.

EXERCISE 1: IDENTIFYING NOUNS

Directions: Circle the nouns in each sentence below.

1. Dan rides a motorcycle to feel the speed.

2. Mr. Archer goes to the stadium because he loves baseball.

3. In Knoxville, Shelley found a new fashion.

4. Aunt Rose finds shells by the ocean.

5. The lawyer paid bail at the courthouse.

6. The president kept a dog in the White House.

Check your work on page 200.

EXERCISE 2: WRITING NOUNS

Directions: Add a noun to each sentence below. Check to see that the nouns you add make sense.

1. _____ was my best friend in school.

2. My _____ thought I was really great.

3. I would like to go on a vacation to _____.

4. The biggest piece of furniture in my home is a _____.

5. The smallest thing I own is a _____.

6. _____ is a quality I admire in people.

Check your work on page 200.

PRONOUNS

Pronouns are words that take the place of nouns.

Pronouns are used like nouns. A pronoun stands for the name of a person, place, thing, or idea. Here are some examples to explain pronouns.

Rosanna got ice cream on Friday. **She** went to the store.

Both sentences talk about Rosanna. But in the second sentence, the pronoun *she* takes the place of the noun *Rosanna*.

Many *cities* get government assistance. **They** use the money for many projects.

Both sentences talk about cities. But in the second sentence, the pronoun *they* takes the place of the noun *cities*.

That **dog** looks hungry. **It** probably hasn't eaten for days.

Both sentences talk about a dog. But in the second sentence, the pronoun *it* takes the place of the noun *dog*.

Many useful pronouns are listed in the box below. You'll be studying these pronouns in this book.

Pronouns
I, me, my, mine
he, him, his
she, her, hers
you, your, yours
we, us, our, ours
they, them, their, theirs
it, its

Find and circle the pronouns in the following sentence.

The landlord wants the rent, and he wants it now.

There are two pronouns in that sentence: *he* and *it*. The pronoun *he* takes the place of *landlord*, and *it* refers to *rent*. Try another example. Check the box of pronouns above if you aren't sure which words are pronouns.

They are leaving town, but all of their friends are staying.

You should have circled the pronouns *they* and *their*.

EXERCISE 3: IDENTIFYING PRONOUNS

Directions: In the following sentences, underline the pronouns.

1. He rides it to feel the speed.

2. He goes to the stadium because he loves baseball.

3. In Knoxville, she found it.

4. She finds them for us by the ocean.

5. He paid bail for me at the courthouse.

6. He kept his dog in the White House.

Check your work on page 200.

EXERCISE 4: WRITING PRONOUNS

Directions: Replace each noun in parentheses with a pronoun. The first one is done as an example.

1. *(The motorcycle)* ___*It*___ has a top speed of 120 mph.

2. *(Mr. Archer)* _____ was a minor league star.

3. *(Shelley's sweaters)* _____ are green and purple.

4. *(Health)* _____ is important whether you are young or old.

5. *(The lawyer)* _____ warned me about getting in trouble again.

6. The president wanted *(his dog)* _____ to behave.

Check your work on page 200.

VERBS

A *verb* is a word that shows action or being.

Some verbs are action words. The verbs in the following sentences show action:

Gloria **painted** her new apartment.
Jim **fixed** the light in the bathroom.

Other verbs are linking (being) verbs. These verbs link a noun or pronoun to words that rename or describe it. These sentences use linking verbs:

Our street **is** very noisy.
The neighbors **are** Sonia and Larry Petrie.

Following are some samples of both kinds of verbs.

Action	Linking
run, go, ride, love, dance, keep, find, fight, pay, drive, drink, laugh	am, is, are, was, were

Those are only a few examples of verbs. There are thousands of verbs. Any time you talk about what something is or does, you use one or more verbs. Read the sentence below and underline each verb you find.

Tilly socializes and dances at parties.

Did you underline the words *socializes* and *dances*? Try another sentence—underline the verb.

This party is wonderful.

You were right if you underlined the word *is*.

EXERCISE 5: IDENTIFYING VERBS

Directions: Underline the verb or verbs in the following sentences.

1. Dan rides a motorcycle to the lake.

2. Mr. Archer goes to the stadium because he is a fan.

3. Shelley found a new fashion when she visited Knoxville.

4. Aunt Rose finds shells by the ocean.

5. The lawyers are at the courthouse.

6. The president kept a dog in the White House.

Check your work on page 200.

EXERCISE 6: WRITING VERBS

Directions: Fill in the blanks with action verbs.

1. List five action verbs that tell what people can do with their legs and

   feet: ___*hop*___, _____, _____, _____, _____.

2. List five action verbs that tell what people can do with their arms and

   hands: ___*sew*___, _____, _____, _____, _____.

3. List five action verbs that tell what people can do with the parts of their

   faces: ___*breathe*___, _____, _____, _____, _____.

4. List five action verbs that tell what people can do with their minds:

   ___*dream*___, _____, _____, _____, _____.

5. List five action verbs that tell what people can do with their whole

   bodies: ___*sleep*___, _____, _____, _____, _____.

Check your work on page 200.

ADJECTIVES

Adjectives describe nouns. They tell which one, what kind, or how many.

You might say to someone, "Meet me by my car." If that person didn't know what your car looked like, he would not be able to meet you. But if you said, "Meet me by the old blue convertible Corvette parked next to the purple shed," he would know exactly which car you meant.

Using adjectives makes a difference. The adjectives *old*, *blue*, and *convertible* describe the Corvette. The adjective *purple* describes the shed. Your friend would be able to find your car because of the specific information that these adjectives provide.

Here are three lists of common adjectives.

What kind	Which one	How many
big, little, young, old, neat, sloppy, happy, sad, nice, kind, red, blue, white	this, that, these, those	many, few, one, two, some

Find and circle the ten adjectives in the following paragraph. All of the adjectives can be found in the box above.

Many people are happy when they see the red, white, and blue flag of the United States. But some people are sad because they think about friends or family who died in a war. Those persons fought and died in big and little wars.

Check to be sure that all the words you circled are on the list. Then count the number of adjectives you found. If you found fewer than ten, look at the list to find the rest.

EXERCISE 7: IDENTIFYING ADJECTIVES

Directions: These sentences contain adjectives that describe nouns or pronouns. Circle all the adjectives in the sentences.

1. Daring Dan rides a red motorcycle to feel the high speed.

2. Mr. Archer goes to the wonderful stadium for exciting games.

3. Shelley discovered a new fashion in fuzzy sweaters.

4. Aunt Rose finds big and little shells by the beautiful ocean.

5. The kind lawyer paid the bail at the old courthouse.

6. The president kept a noisy dog in the busy White House.

Check your work on page 200.

EXERCISE 8: WRITING ADJECTIVES

Directions: List five adjectives that describe each of the following.

You	Your home	Your father
1. _____	_____	_____
2. _____	_____	_____
3. _____	_____	_____
4. _____	_____	_____
5. _____	_____	_____

Check your work on page 200.

ADVERBS

Adverbs describe verbs. Adverbs can tell how, when, or where.

To begin to study how adverbs work, look at the following sentence.

He writes.

In that sentence, you know that the person writes, but you don't know anything about *how* he writes. Read the next sentence.

He writes **neatly**.

In that sentence, you learn how he writes. The adverb *neatly* describes the verb *writes*. Now look at another sentence.

He writes **daily.**

In that sentence, you know *when* he writes. The adverb *daily* describes the verb *writes*. As you can see, an adverb often comes right after the verb it describes. Look at one more sentence.

He writes **here.**

In that sentence, you know *where* he writes. The adverb *here* describes the verb *writes*.

In the following sentences, the verbs have been underlined and the adverbs circled. Answer the questions that follow each sentence. They will help you understand how adverbs are used. The first one has been done for you as an example.

The judge <u>arrived</u> (late.)

What did he do? ___arrived___

When did he do it? ___late___

The trial <u>began</u> (immediately.)

What did it do? _____

When did it do it? _____

The victim <u>sobbed</u> (quietly.)

What did she do? _____

How did she do it? _____

The jury just <u>sat</u> (there.)

What did the jury do? _____

Where did they do it? _____

The judge <u>looked</u> (angrily) at the suspect.

What did he do? _____

How did he do it? _____

EXERCISE 9: IDENTIFYING ADVERBS

Directions: Underline the adverbs in the following sentences. Remember, an adverb tells how, when, or where.

1. Uncle Dan rides dangerously. *(How does he ride?)*

2. Mr. Archer arrives early. *(When does he arrive?)*

3. Shelley bought her sweater there. *(Where did she buy it?)*

4. Aunt Rose looked carefully. *(How did she look?)*

5. The lawyer paid immediately. *(When did he pay?)*

6. The president's dog barked loudly. *(How did it bark?)*

Check your work on page 200.

EXERCISE 10: WRITING ADVERBS

Directions: Complete the following sentences by writing in adverbs that tell how, when, or where. You can choose adverbs from the following list, or you can think of your own.

sweetly, daily, upstairs, now, there, wildly, constantly, quickly, outdoors

1. *(how)* Caroline sings _____.

2. *(when)* Caroline sings _____.

3. *(where)* Caroline sings _____.

4. *(how)* The kitten plays _____.

5. *(when)* The kitten plays _____.

6. *(where)* The kitten plays _____.

Check your work on page 200.

EXERCISE 11: CHAPTER REVIEW

You have had a quick overview of five parts of speech. As you work through this book, you will continue to study nouns, pronouns, verbs, adjectives, and adverbs. You will have a very good understanding of them when you finish the book.

The next two exercises are a review of this chapter. Look up any information you need to complete the exercises.

Part 1

Directions: Twenty-five words are listed at the beginning of this exercise. Decide what part of speech each word is. Write each word in the correct column. The first row has been completed for you.

early, neat, Mr. Archer, listens, he, red, they, there, slowly, dog, happy, keep, angrily, went, you, baseball, find, now, loves, motorcycle, old, boat, it, me, nice

	Nouns	Pronouns	Verbs	Adjectives	Adverbs
1.	Mr. Archer	he	listens	neat	early
2.					
3.					
4.					
5.					

Part 2

Directions: Add a word to fill in each blank. After the sentence, tell whether you used a noun, pronoun, verb, adjective, or adverb.

                                                              Part of Speech

1. Dan rode his _____ to the lake.   _____

2. Mr. Archer _____ to the stadium.   _____

3. Shelley told me about her _____ sweater.   _____

4. Aunt Rose looked _____ for shells.   _____

5. The dog ate _____ dinner.   _____

Check your work on pages 200–201.

YOUR TURN TO WRITE
AN EVENT IN YOUR LIFE

You have already done some writing in this book. When you wrote in your journal, you wrote something private—just for yourself. You didn't have to worry about writing neatly and correctly because no one else reads your journal.

Now you are going to do a different kind of writing assignment. This assignment asks you to write a paragraph. As you write, keep in mind that others will want to be able to understand your writing. Make your writing as clear and correct as you can.

You will have many writing assignments in this book. Keep all your writing assignments in a notebook or folder. Do not use your journal, since your journal is just for you. As you work through the book, you will be able to reread your assignments and see how your writing is improving.

WRITING ASSIGNMENT

Directions: Put the date at the top of this first assignment and every writing assignment. You will have a record of when you did the writing.

For this assignment, write a story about an event in your life. When writing a story, it's easiest to start with the first thing that happened and write down all the information in time order.

You may write about anything that happened to you, whether it was a very important event in your life or just something that happened the other day. If you're stuck and can't think of anything to write about, you could try to start writing by using freewriting.

Below are some suggestions for topics:

My first job	My favorite day
The day I almost died	A vacation to . . .
The first time I drove	My best/worst childhood memory

You can choose a different topic to write on. Just be sure to pick a topic that really interests you.

☑ Writing Checklist

- ❑ Have you said all you wanted to say?
- ❑ Are there any changes you want to make?
- ❑ Did you put a date at the top of the writing?

CHAPTER 2

JOURNAL WRITING
CLUSTERING

Putting your thoughts down can be a little difficult at times. You might feel like writing but find that you don't know where to start. One way to begin writing is to make a word cluster. Just as grapes cluster together, your brain clusters thoughts and ideas. Making a word cluster can help you come up with new writing ideas.

Clustering means writing one word in the middle of the page and jotting down all the thoughts that come to your mind on the page around that first word. Don't try to write sentences. Begin by writing words.

An example of clustering follows. The subject is FAMILY. Here are the instructions the writer followed to make the cluster:

1. Write the word FAMILY in the middle of the paper and circle the word.
2. In the space around the word FAMILY, write down any words that pop into your mind on the subject of family and circle those words.
3. Draw arrows connecting the words that seem to go together.
4. Continue doing this until you are ready to write.
5. Write sentences using some or all of the words from the cluster.

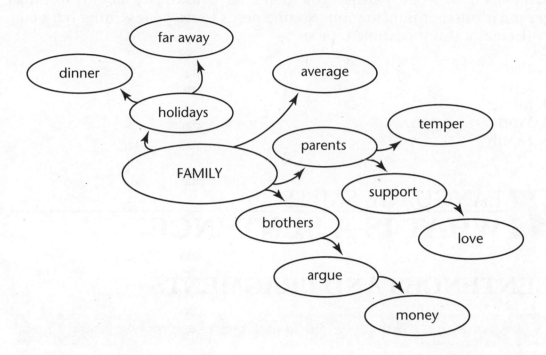

Notice all the circles around the words. Look at the arrows that the writer joined words with. Could some of those words be put together to form ideas and sentences? You never have to use all the words in a cluster—just the ones that give you something to say.

Here are the sentences the writer wrote after making the cluster.

> I live with a fairly average family. My parents and I get along, but my dad also has a very bad temper. We may fight sometimes, but they're always there to offer their love and support. My brothers and I don't argue as much anymore because they both live far away now. That makes it hard for the whole family to get together for dinner during the holidays.

Clustering works very well for some people. Try it a couple of times and see if it works for you. If you don't like it, you are always welcome to choose another method to get going when you start writing.

JOURNAL ENTRY

Directions: Your entry will be a group of sentences. You can write on any topic that interests you. If there's nothing in particular that you want to write about, you can choose from the topics listed on the next page. Start writing after you've decided on a topic and write until you have nothing else to say. If you don't know where to start, begin with a word cluster. Your thoughts will tell you when it is time to begin writing your sentences.

Remember, in your journal you don't have to worry about spelling, grammar rules, or punctuation. No one needs to see your writing but you.

Here is a list of possible topics:

1. War
2. Love
3. Money
4. Work
5. Family

 LANGUAGE SKILLS
WHAT IS A SENTENCE?

SENTENCES AND FRAGMENTS

A *sentence* is a group of words that expresses a complete thought.

The words in a sentence make sense. You can understand what the writer is saying. Is the following group of words a sentence?

The man was driving very fast.

That group of words tells a complete thought, so it is a sentence. What about the next group of words?

Pulled out behind him.

Those words do not tell a complete thought. Something is missing. The second group of words is a fragment.

A *fragment* does not express a complete thought.

A fragment leaves a question in your mind. In the example you just saw, *who* pulled out behind him? Some information was left out of the sentence. Information can be added to a fragment to make it a complete thought:

The police pulled out behind him.

Now you have a complete thought. Now you have a sentence. You can understand what writers are saying when they use complete sentences.

Here are some more examples of complete sentences.

The police stopped the speeding car.
The driver was drunk.
The police arrested him for drunk driving.

Each one of those sentences made sense and told a complete thought. You could understand what was being said.

Now look at some examples of fragments.

After the game.
Ori's party.
Too many people.
Left early.

When you read the fragments above, you might realize that someone is talking about a party, but a lot of information is left out. What happened *after the game*? What about *Ori's party*?

Information can be added to the fragments so that they express complete thoughts. Read the sentences below and compare them with the fragments.

After the game, I wanted to have a good time.
At eight o'clock I was at Ori's party.
There were too many people there.
Ori's house was so crowded that I left early.

Complete the Following

A sentence expresses a _____ _____.

A fragment _____ express a _____ _____.

EXERCISE 1: IDENTIFYING SENTENCES AND FRAGMENTS

Directions: Read the following sentences and fragments. In the blank after each group of words, write *S* if it is a sentence or *F* if it is a fragment.

1. April is a mixed-up month. ___*S*___

2. Income taxes. _____

3. Often celebrate Easter. _____

4. Jewish families often celebrate Passover. _____

5. In one week. _____

6. The weather is warm. _____

7. Sometimes it snows. _____

8. One day the sun is out. _____

9. Next day snow. _____

10. Do I like April because I'm mixed up too? _____

Check your work on page 201.

EXERCISE 2: TURNING FRAGMENTS INTO SENTENCES

Directions: Each of the following groups of words is a fragment. After each fragment, you will find a question. Answer the question by writing a complete sentence. Use the fragment and add some new information to write your answer. The first one is done as an example.

1. Took the man to jail. *(Who took the man to jail?)*

   The police took the man to jail.

2. Was very angry. *(Who was very angry?)*

   _____

3. Locked him up. *(Who locked him up?)*

   _____

4. His lawyer. *(How did he contact his lawyer?)*

   _____

5. Stayed in jail overnight. *(Who stayed in jail?)*

   _____

6. Sleep in jail. *(How did he feel about sleeping in jail?)*

   _____

7. Felt terrible. *(Who or what felt terrible?)*

   _____

Check your work on page 201.

PUNCTUATING PERFECTLY

WHAT DOES A SENTENCE LOOK LIKE?

A sentence is a group of words that tells a complete thought. It is also a group of words that has a special look. If you look closely at all the sentences in this book, you'll see that they both begin and end in a certain way.

Here is an opportunity for you to do a little detective work about sentences. Look closely at the sentences on this page and then answer the following questions.

What kind of letter does the first word of each sentence begin with?

_____

What marks do you find at the ends of the sentences?

_____

Did you discover that the first word of each sentence begins with a capital letter? Did you discover that there are punctuation marks at the end of each sentence?

You need to remember these two rules when writing a sentence:

1. The first word of each sentence begins with a capital letter.
2. Each sentence ends with a punctuation mark. This will be one of three endmarks: a period (.), a question mark (?), or an exclamation point (!).

Read on to find out more about when to use these endmarks.

EVERY SENTENCE HAS A PURPOSE

There are four different types of sentences. The first type makes a statement (gives information). The second type gives a command (tells someone to do something). The third type asks a question. The fourth type is an exclamation (shows strong feeling). Here are examples of all four types. Notice how each begins with a capital letter and ends with an endmark.

STATEMENT: I want to go bowling.
COMMAND: Take me to the bowling lanes.
QUESTION: Did you get my bowling shoes?
EXCLAMATION: Good grief, I lost again!

Statements

Most of the sentences that you write or read are statements. They give you information about a subject. They end with a period. Look at the following statement.

Janet bought four bags of groceries.

That group of words gives you information about Janet's shopping. It is a complete thought, and it ends with a period.

Write an example of a statement on the line below.

_____

Commands

Commands tell someone to do something. As you have grown up, you have heard a lot of commands from parents and teachers and also brothers and sisters. Do these sound familiar?

Clean your room.   Brush your teeth.
Be home by midnight.   Take your hands off my radio.
Shut the door.

Can you think of any commands that you heard again and again? If so, jot them down on the next two lines.

_____

_____

In writing, a command often looks like a statement because a command usually ends with a period. However, the two types of sentences are different. A statement just gives information. In a command, the writer is telling the reader to do something. You can mentally fill in the missing word *you* in a command. Here are some examples:

(You) Clean your room.   *(You)* Feed the dog.
(You) Wash the car.   *(You)* Be home by dark.

Questions

A question is very easy to identify. It *asks* something, and it ends with a question mark. You ask many questions each day. Here are some examples of common questions.

What time is it?   How are you?
What's for dinner?   Where's the sugar?
Did the mail come?   Where is my change?

On the lines below, write three questions you asked at some time today.

_____

_____

_____

Do all your questions ask for information? Does each end with a question mark?

Exclamations

An exclamation shows strong feeling. It ends with an exclamation point. Exclamations are often made at exciting or frightening times. Here are some sentences that are exclamations. Notice that they all end with exclamation points.

It's a touchdown!   You just won $100,000,000!
That dress is gorgeous!   Look out for that car!
Mommy's home!   Let's celebrate!

Notice that one of the exclamations—Look out for that car!—is a command that is said with strong feeling.

On the line below, write a sentence that is an exclamation. You might want to think of one you used at a game, at a party, or when you accidentally touched a hot stove.

_____

Do you have an exclamation point at the end of the sentence?

EXERCISE 3: TYPES OF SENTENCES

Directions: Read each of the following sentences. Place the correct endmark (period, question mark, or exclamation point) at the end of each sentence. Then, on the line next to the sentence, write whether the sentence is a statement, a command, a question, or an exclamation. The first one is done as an example.

1. This is the Rainbow Coffee Shop ___.___ _statement_

2. Would you like to see a menu _____ _____

3. Get me a glass of water _____ _____

4. The food here is supposed to be awful _____ _____

5. Do you smell smoke coming from the kitchen _____ _____

6. This place is on fire _____ _____

Check your work on page 201.

EXERCISE 4: MISTAKES IN SENTENCES

Directions: Each of the following sentences may contain mistakes in punctuation or capitalization. Some may be fragments. Rewrite each sentence correctly. The first one is done as an example.

1. Sky-high rents.

   The rents here are sky-high.

2. it is difficult to find a new apartment.

   _____

3. Why did they have to tear our building down.

   _____

4. Only three months till.

   _____

5. most landlords won't permit pets.

   _____

6. Can't give up my dog!

   _____

Check your work on page 201.

PUTTING YOUR SKILLS TO WORK

Directions: This assignment is for your writing folder or notebook. Keep all your new skills for writing correct sentences in mind as you do this assignment.

Write eight sentences. Write two sentences of each kind that you have just studied. After each sentence, indicate whether it is a statement, a command, a question, or an exclamation.

You can write your sentences about any topic you wish. When you are finished writing, reread your sentences and check them against this checklist.

☑ Writing Checklist

❏ Does each sentence begin with a capital letter and end with an endmark?

❏ Do you have two examples of all four different kinds of sentences? Did you use endmarks correctly for each kind?

EVERY SENTENCE HAS A SUBJECT

The *subject* of a sentence is the person, place, thing, or idea talked about in the sentence. The sentence will tell what the subject does or is.

To find the subject of a sentence, look for the verb in the sentence. If the verb shows action, figure out who or what is performing the action. In the following sentence, what is the action verb? Who performs the action?

The dentist pulled all of my wisdom teeth.

In that sentence, the action verb is *pulled*. The person performing the pulling is the dentist, so *The dentist* is the subject.

Here is another example. What is the action verb? Who performs the action?

The receptionist made another appointment for me.

The verb in that sentence is *made*. The receptionist is performing the action of the verb, so *The receptionist* is the subject.

When the verb in a sentence doesn't show action, it is a linking verb. In that case, ask yourself, "Who or what is this sentence about?" Here's an example:

My mouth was numb for three hours.

The verb *was* is a linking verb. The sentence is about the writer's mouth, so *my mouth* is the subject.

Complete the Following

On the lines below, explain what the subject of a sentence is. You may go back to the beginning of the section if you need help with the explanation.

_____

_____

EXERCISE 5: FINDING THE SUBJECT

Directions: In each of the following sentences, first find the verb and underline it. Then circle the subject. The first one is done as an example.

1. (Chicago) is a big city.

2. People live in interesting neighborhoods.

3. Trains take many workers downtown.

4. The buildings are tall there.

5. The wind blows hard in the winter.

6. People hurry to the train stations.

7. Workers ride home on the trains.

Check your work on page 201.

TRICKY SUBJECTS
Commands and Questions

So far you have seen that the subject of a sentence can come right at the beginning of the sentence. However, the subject can be in many places. Sometimes the way a sentence is written makes finding the subject hard.

When you studied commands, you learned that you can always add the missing word *you* to a command. In fact, the subject of a command is always the missing *you*. Here's an example:

> Write a letter to your aunt.
> *(You)* Write a letter to your aunt.

The missing *you* is the subject of the sentence.

In a question, part of the verb often comes before the subject. To find the subject, mentally put the sentence back in order as if it were a statement. Here's an example:

> Did Adele write a letter to her aunt?

Put the sentence in order as if it were a statement instead of a question:

> Adele did write a letter to her aunt.

Now you can tell that *Adele* is the subject of the sentence because she is performing the action.

Try another example. Here is a question. Mentally rearrange the question so that it is a statement. Then find the subject.

Has the president signed the bill?

Here is the question, rearranged as a statement:

The president has signed the bill.

The subject performing the action is *The president.*

Confusing Words and Phrases

Sometimes extra words and phrases in a sentence can confuse you when you are looking for the subject. Remember always to look for the verb. If it is an action verb, who or what is performing the action? If it is a linking verb, who or what is the sentence about?

In the following sentence, words come between the subject and the verb. What is the verb? What is the subject?

The women in the bathroom giggle.

The verb is *giggle.* The performer of the action is *The women.* The words *in the bathroom* come between the subject and the verb. Your common sense will help you with a sentence like this. Obviously, a bathroom cannot giggle, so the subject cannot be *the bathroom*!

Now try another example. The following sentence starts out with some words that are not the subject. Find the verb; then find the subject.

In this park, the trees are tall and old.

The verb is *are,* a linking verb. The subject is *the trees.* The verb links the words *tall and old* to *trees.*

EXERCISE 6: FINDING TRICKY SUBJECTS

Directions: Write the subject of each sentence in the blank. Remember that the subject could be the missing *you.* The first one is done as an example.

1. Does Denise come in today? ___*Denise*___

2. On Tuesdays, Sarah takes her place. _____

3. Give Sarah a coffee break at 10:00. _____

4. Larry, the typist on the left, drinks tea. _____

5. Is the coffee ready to drink? _____

6. Put some water on for tea. _____

7. At 10:00, we go to the lounge. _____

8. The workers in the lounge watch game shows. _____

9. Change the channel, please. _____

10. Would you like to join us?_____

Check your work on page 201.

EXERCISE 7: WRITING SUBJECTS

Directions: Add subjects to the following sentences.

1. _____ is my hometown.

2. _____ is the name of the local paper.

3. In an emergency, _____ is the best hospital.

4. For bargain prices, _____ beats all the stores in town.

5. _____ has plants in his house.

6. Sometimes _____ giggles too much.

7. In my opinion, a _____ looks nicer than any other car.

Check your work on page 201.

EVERY SENTENCE HAS A PREDICATE

The subject is one important part of a sentence. The predicate is the other important part. It's not hard to find the predicate. Everything that isn't part of the subject is part of the predicate.

> The *predicate* of a sentence tells what the subject does or is.

The predicate gives information about the subject. There is always a verb in the predicate. Look at this sentence, which contains an action verb.

The mechanic replaced the car's muffler.

There are two parts to that sentence. *The mechanic* is the subject. The predicate is *replaced the car's muffler*. The subject is the person who completed the action. The predicate tells what the subject did.

Now look at the next sentence, which contains a linking verb.

The muffler is expensive.

There are also two parts to that sentence. *The muffler* is the subject. The predicate is *is expensive*. In that sentence, the predicate tells what the subject is.

EXERCISE 8: WRITING ACTION PREDICATES

Directions: Ten one-word subjects are listed below. One-word predicates have been added to the first two. Add one-word predicates to the last eight subjects. Use verbs that tell what the subjects do. (When there is only one word in a predicate, it will always be a verb.)

1. Babies ____*cry*____.

2. Smoke ____*rises*____.

3. Parrots _____.

4. Flowers _____.

5. Cats _____.

6. Dogs _____.

7. Birds _____.

8. Fish _____.

9. Mosquitoes _____.

10. Scissors _____.

Check your work on page 202.

EXERCISE 9: WRITING LINKING PREDICATES

Directions: Add two-word predicates to these subjects. One of the words must be a verb. Use linking verbs to tell what the subjects are.

1. Mary __*is*__ ___*happy*___.

2. The tomatoes ___*are*___ ___*red*___.

3. The pool __*is*__ ___*open*___

4. My apartment ____ _____.

5. Bicycles ____ _____.

6. The dog ____ _____.

7. Dad ____ _____.

8. His motorcycle ____ _____.

9. Our money ____ _____.

10. Summer ____ _____.

Check your work on page 202.

PUTTING YOUR SKILLS TO WORK

Directions: You've learned a lot about sentences so far in this chapter. Now you'll have a chance to put what you've learned into writing—in a paragraph about someone you know. Put this writing assignment in your writing folder or notebook. Write carefully and correctly so that others will be able to understand your writing.

Write a paragraph about someone you know. First, name the person and tell how you know him or her. Second, tell where you spend time together. Third, tell what you do when you spend time together. Finally, tell why you enjoy being with this person.

☑ Writing Checklist

❑ Do you have a subject for each sentence?
❑ Do you have a predicate for each sentence?

THE SUBJECTS OF YOUR LIFE

There are a great many important people, places, and things in your life. You can think of them as the subjects of your life. The most important subjects for you might be your family, your friends, your home, your work, your education, and your activities. You are going to make your own personalized spelling list. Put this assignment in the back of your writing notebook or folder.

Write the heading "The Subjects of My Life" at the top of the page. Complete the following lists with the names of people, places, or things (nouns). The names on the list will be capitalized, since the name of any specific person, place, or thing must begin with a capital letter. For example, *brother* is not capitalized, but *Joe* is. You don't capitalize *state*, but you capitalize *Maryland*.

This will be your personalized, capitalized spelling list. If an area does not apply to you, skip it. If you are not sure of the spelling of a name, check with someone and get the right spelling before you write it down. You can use this list to check for correct spelling whenever you write about yourself and your family and friends.

The Subjects of My Life

People

mother	*Mildred Levy*	boyfriend	*Brian Van Slyke*
father	*Bernard Levy*	girlfriend	
sister(s)	*Velma Levy*	fiancé (man)	
	Alice Levy	fiancée (woman)	

People

mother _____

father _____

sister(s) _____

_____

brother(s) _____

_____

grandfather _____

grandmother _____

friend(s) _____

_____

teacher_____

boyfriend _____

girlfriend _____

fiancé (man) _____

fiancée (woman) _____

aunt(s) _____

_____

uncle(s) _____

_____

nephew_____

niece _____

cousin _____

Places

street _____

school _____

city _____

county _____

state _____

place of work _____

road _____

restaurant _____

park _____

shopping center _____

Things

book _____

team _____

soft drink _____

car _____

athletic shoes _____

candy bar _____

☑ Spelling Checklist

❏ Is everything spelled correctly?
❏ Does every word start with a capital letter? They all should, because they all name specific persons, places, or things.

All the words in this list have a special meaning to you. In the future, when you use these words, stop and think about the spelling. Make sure you have spelled them correctly.

Complete the following paragraph. Use words from your personalized, capitalized spelling list.

I have lived in _____ for _____ years.
                        (state)   (number)

I live on _____ in _____.
                    (street)   (town or city)

_____ and _____
     (names of people in your home)

live with me. Many of my days are the same. I get up in the

morning and go to _____. When I
                              (work or school)

get there, _____ tells me what
                        (boss or teacher)

I have to do for the day After a hard day, I sometimes stop to

buy a _____ and _____.
              (soft drink)   (candy)

I know that eating so much sugar is bad for me, but I do it

anyhow. After all, there are worse vices.

EXERCISE 10: CHAPTER REVIEW

Part 1
Directions: Fill in the blanks in the following paragraphs.

1. Every sentence has _____ parts. They are

    the _____ and the _____. In sentences, the

    _____ is a person, place, thing, or idea, and verbs are used in

    the _____.

2. There are four types of sentences. A sentence that simply says something

    is a _____. A sentence that demands that something be done

    is a _____. A sentence that asks something is a _____.

    And a sentence that shows very strong emotion is an _____.

Part 2

Directions: Write the subject of each of the following sentences in the blanks. The first one is done as an example.

1. Juan wants to find a job. _____ *Juan* _____

2. A counselor in the unemployment office helps him. _____

3. Each week, Juan goes on at least one job interview. _____

4. Will this company hire Juan? _____

5. The interviewer talked to the manager. _____

6. Give Juan a chance. _____

7. Can Rona train him next week? _____

Part 3

Directions: Read the following five groups of sentences. Four of the five sentences in each group contain one or more mistakes. Circle the letter of the correct sentence in each group.

1. a. going back to school is not easy
   b. Students need time to study?
   c. Once the brain is out of gear.
   d. It is difficult to start thinking again.
   e. takes determination.

2. a. College is not like high school.
   b. no detention!
   c. we can talk.
   d. teachers are human?
   e. We like it

3. a. In high school my grades
   b. Knew I was smart.
   c. I hated to study.
   d. teachers didn't like me?
   e. If I try, I can do it

4. a. Argue all the time.
   b. Sometimes I yell at them.
   c. i think they fight too much.
   d. Don't want them to argue
   e. Want them to stop.

5. a. When I was playing volleyball.
   b. my knee hit the ground hard
   c. Took me to the emergency room?
   d. X rays.
   e. Now I have a plaster cast.

Part 4

Directions: Look at the four pictures on this page. Under each picture, write two things:

❏ what is happening in the picture

❏ what the characters in the pictures might be saying

Try to write at least one of each of the four types of sentences.

1. _____

_____

2. _____

_____

3. _____

_____

4. _____

_____

Check your work on page 202.

YOUR TURN TO WRITE
MAKING A WORD PICTURE

When you want to describe something to another person who can't see the thing you're describing, you need to use a lot of details. For example, if you wrote in a letter to a friend, "The park near our new house is beautiful," your friend would know your opinion, but she would not be able to imagine what the park looked like. Realizing that you need to add more details, you might write something like this:

> The park near our new house is beautiful. It's a block long, and there are trees all around the edges. In the very center of the park is a garden with fragrant flowers. The park is very quiet and peaceful.

The details you added would be the things you could see, hear, and smell in the park. When you include details, you need to think about what you can see, hear, smell, feel, and even taste.

WRITING ASSIGNMENT

Directions: This assignment is for your writing folder or notebook. Remember to date the assignment. Use your spelling list from page 39 for this writing. You may even be adding a few new words to the list. Write carefully and correctly, using all the writing skills you have learned.

Write a paragraph telling about one of four things:

1. Your writing classroom
2. The place where you relax
3. A place you visit often
4. Your choice

You might want to include the name of the place and the names of the people you see there. You could also explain what you do there and mention the days you are there.

✓ Writing Checklist

❏ Have you checked your spelling?
❏ Have you written complete sentences?
❏ Is the first letter of every sentence capitalized?
❏ Is there a punctuation mark at the end of every sentence?

CHAPTER 3

JOURNAL WRITING
WHAT'S ON YOUR MIND?

Write that letter, but don't mail it!

What's troubling you? Is something causing you to lose sleep? to lose money? to feel guilty? Are you irritated because you are the only person in your home doing the evening chores while everyone else watches TV? Has a friend jokingly insulted you one time too many?

What's on your mind?

JOURNAL ENTRY

Directions: You now have the opportunity to vent stored-up anger, frustration, and hostility without damaging any relationships. Write that person a letter—in your journal. Say anything and everything you've always wanted to say.

Start out with "Dear _____" and keep writing. Describe what upsets you. Tell the person anything you want. And then, don't mail the letter. You will have spoken your piece. Once you put all your thoughts down and read what you've said, you might find you are capable of taking some action about the situation.

Of course, if you don't feel like writing a letter right now, you're free to write a journal entry on any topic that interests you.

Remember, your journal is just for you. You don't have to worry about correct grammar or spelling when you write a journal entry—just put your thoughts on paper.

44

LANGUAGE SKILLS
NOUNS AND PRONOUNS

Nouns and pronouns are both naming words. They tell you whom or what someone else is talking or writing about. You use them to tell whom or what you are talking or writing about.

Here's a demonstration of how important nouns and pronouns are. In the following paragraph, the nouns and pronouns have been replaced with blanks.

Without _____ _____ would be impossible

to talk about _____ , _____ , _____ , or _____ .

How could _____ talk about _____ _____

if _____ or _____ didn't have a _____?

Now look at the same paragraph with the nouns and pronouns filled in.

Without **nouns it** would be impossible to talk about **people**, **places**, **things**, or **ideas**. How could **you** talk about **your neighbor** if **he** or **she** didn't have a **name**?

Here are some examples of nouns and pronouns to refresh your memory.

NOUNS: daughter, Los Angeles, truth, spoon,
Jim Smith, lake, car
PRONOUNS: he, she, it, they, you, we, us

Get the idea? Without nouns and pronouns, it is impossible to communicate. As naming words, nouns and pronouns are very similar. They both identify a person, place, thing, or idea.

Before we really get down to work in this chapter, see if you remember the definitions of nouns and pronouns from Chapter 1.

Complete the Following

A noun names a _____, _____, _____,

or _____.

A pronoun takes the _____ of a _____.

Did you remember? Whether you did or didn't, just read on.

NOUNS

As you learned in Chapter 1, a noun names a person, place, thing, or idea. Nouns identify who or what is being talked about. In this section of the book, you will work with several types of nouns. In the following exercise, review what you already know about nouns.

EXERCISE 1: IDENTIFYING NOUNS

Directions: In the following paragraph, underline all of the nouns. The first two have been underlined for you as examples.

> <u>Nan</u> loves her <u>dog</u>, Fifi. Fifi is a poodle. At the beach, Nan wants to be certain that Fifi does not get too hot. Nan bought a stroller with an awning so Fifi could be in the shade while on the beach. Nan also often buys ice cream for Fifi. Many people on the beach stare at the poodle. The people also stare at Nan!

Check your work on page 202.

COMMON NOUNS AND PROPER NOUNS

You will be working with two types of nouns in this chapter: common nouns and proper nouns. Both types of nouns name persons, places, things, or ideas. But there is an important difference between common and proper nouns.

> A **common noun** is the *general* name of a person, place, thing, or idea.
> A **proper noun** is the *specific* name of a person, place, thing, or idea.

Words like *woman, building, airplane,* and *month* are common nouns. Words like *Lynn, Empire State Building, Concorde,* and *December* are proper nouns.

A common noun never begins with a capital letter (unless it comes at the beginning of a sentence). A proper noun, on the other hand, always begins with a capital letter. Here is an example of a common noun and a proper noun.

COMMON NOUN: city
PROPER NOUN: Detroit

The common noun is *city* because it names a general type of place. You could be talking about any city in the world. But *Detroit* is a specific place, so it is a proper noun. Notice that *Detroit* begins with a capital letter, while *city* does not.

To get a better understanding of common nouns and proper nouns, study the lists below. Notice that, for each common noun on the left, there is a corresponding proper noun on the right.

Common Nouns	Proper Nouns
school	Roosevelt High
car	Chevrolet
singer	Whitney Houston
store	K-Mart
restaurant	Mama Leone's
day	Friday
actor	Tom Cruise

When you are deciding whether a noun is a common noun or a proper noun, remember that a common noun is a general name, while a proper noun is a specific name.

When you are writing proper nouns of more than one word, you usually capitalize all the words. For example, suppose that you are writing the name of a restaurant. You would write *Country Kitchen*, not *Country kitchen*.

EXERCISE 2: COMMON AND PROPER NOUNS

Directions: Below is a list of common nouns. Write the name of a proper noun for each common noun. The first two are done as examples.

1. car: *Honda*

2. boy: *Tommy*

3. lake: _____

4. senator: _____

5. company: _____

6. street: _____

7. town: _____

8. minister: _____

9. holiday: _____

10. state: _____

11. country: _____

12. organization: _____

13. county: _____

14. doctor: _____

Check your work on pages 202–203.

Specific Names

Sometimes it is difficult to decide whether to use a common noun or a proper noun. In fact, many nouns can be either common or proper. The way they are used will tell you which they are.

Words that are used as the specific names of people are proper nouns. However, titles like *senator, doctor, judge, sergeant, vice president, lieutenant, pastor*, and *mayor* are common nouns when they refer to the position. For example, you would write

Kate Jordan is a **senator**.

In that sentence, the word *senator* is used as a job title. It names a position, so it is not capitalized. But you would write

Many people admire **Senator Kate Jordan**.

In that sentence, *Senator* is used as part of a specific name, so the word *Senator* is capitalized. Titles are capitalized when they are used as part of a name.

Words that refer to places or things can also be common nouns or proper nouns. Words like *building, school, department*, and *road* are capitalized when they are used as part of a name. Look at the example below.

My sister goes to **Field School**.
Did she go to **school** today?

In the first sentence, the word *School* is used as part of a name, so it is capitalized. Since *school* is not used as part of a name in the second sentence, it is not capitalized.

Now look at the following sentences. Capitalize all of the proper nouns.

I went to the doctor.
The nurse said, "doctor rahji will be ten minutes late."
"The doctor had to stop at mercy hospital," the nurse
added.
"How far away is the hospital?" I asked.
"It's about two miles down the road," the nurse said.
Just then, a sergeant walked into the office.
"Oh, sergeant jones, you're early," said the nurse.
"There wasn't much traffic on willow road," the
sergeant explained.

Look back at your work. You should have capitalized *Doctor Rahji, Mercy Hospital, Sergeant Jones*, and *Willow Road*. These are proper nouns because they are used as the names of specific people and places.

EXERCISE 3: CAPITALIZING PROPER NOUNS

Directions: Read the following sentences. If all of the proper nouns in a sentence are capitalized, write *C* for *Correct* in the blank. If you find a proper noun that should be capitalized, underline it. Some sentences contain more than one proper noun. The first one is done as an example.

_____ 1. Mrs. Linkowski first saw the <u>washington monument</u> when she was five.

_____ 2. If Tim has those symptoms again, call doctor lee.

_____ 3. New year's eve is aunt Betty's favorite holiday.

_____ 4. My car is a ford escort.

_____ 5. Sam's favorite rock groups are the rolling stones and the grateful dead.

_____ 6. The teachers at brookmont elementary school wrote a letter to mayor carlson.

_____ 7. My dentist hasn't missed a green bay packers game in seven years.

_____ 8. Who ran for mayor in the last election?

_____ 9. Ms. Davis is a member of an organization called mothers against drunk driving.

_____ 10. The oak valley fire department was too late to save the warehouse.

Check your work on page 203.

Complete the Following

In your own words, tell the difference between common nouns

and proper nouns. _____

_____

_____

SINGULAR NOUNS AND PLURAL NOUNS

Nouns that name one person, place, or thing are called *singular nouns.*
Nouns that name more than one person, place, or thing are called
plural nouns.

Here are some examples:

Singular Nouns	Plural Nouns
bird	birds
husband	husbands
class	classes
child	children

The following sentences show some ways that singular and plural nouns
are used.

You have one **bird** now, but after the eggs hatch, you will
have five **birds.**
It is legal to have one **husband** but illegal to have two
husbands.
Sharon is taking one science **class** this year, but next year
she will take two science **classes.**
Erma wants to have one **child**, but Steve wants her to have
six **children.**

FORMING PLURALS

There are several rules for making singular nouns plural. Study and
practice the following rules to make sure you know how to form plural
nouns correctly.

1. The usual way to make singular nouns plural is to add an *s.* Here are
    some examples. Study them carefully and then complete the second
    and third rows.

    planet—planets   flower—flowers   balloon—balloons

    book— _____   cake— _____   clown— _____

    monkey— _____   play— _____   toy— _____

2. Nouns that end in *s, sh, ch, z,* and *x* have *es* added to the end when they are plural. Study these examples and complete the second row.

    bus—buses   box—boxes   church—churches

    dish— _____   waltz— _____ branch— _____

3. Nouns that end in the letter *y* with a consonant before the *y* are made plural by changing the *y* to an *i* and adding *es*. Some examples follow. Study them, and then complete the second row.

    county—counties   salary—salaries   city—cities

    country— _____   enemy— _____   bully— _____

4. Some nouns do not change form at all when they are plural. If you are ever unsure about whether to change the form of a noun to make it plural, you can check the dictionary. Here are some examples of nouns whose singular and plural forms are the same.

    sheep   deer   fish

5. The plurals of some nouns are not formed according to any set of rules. The only way to learn them is to memorize them. Do you know the plural form for the following nouns? The first row has been done for you. If there are any you don't know, look up the singular form in a dictionary.

    child—children   goose—geese   man—men

    woman— _____   mouse— _____   ox— _____

    tooth— _____   louse— _____   foot— _____

EXERCISE 4: CHANGING SINGULAR NOUNS TO PLURAL

Directions: Read the following sentences. In each sentence, cross out the singular noun that should be plural and write the plural form above it. The first one is done as an example.

1. Many ~~woman~~ *women* do not want to work outside the home.

2. They feel that all child should be reared by their mothers.

3. A lot of book say it is not right for women to work.

4. Some woman argue that they must work to earn money.

5. Some employer pay women less than men.

6. Salary should be the same for all people who do the same job.

7. Some companies have child care program.

8. Often, several church in a town have day care centers.

9. Many school bus will pick students up at the centers.

10. City, counties, and towns should do even more to help mothers who must work.

Check your work on page 203.

EXERCISE 5: CORRECTING ERRORS WITH NOUNS

Directions: There is one mistake in each group of sentences below. The mistakes have to do with the use of either singular and plural nouns or common and proper nouns. Read each group of sentences and show which sentence is *not* correct by shading in the box under a, b, or c in the answers.

	a	b	c
1. a. Hunger is widespread. b. Many people eat only one meals a day. c. Some people do not even get one meal.	☐	☐	☐
2. a. What can an american do about the problem? b. She can support her local food bank. c. Food banks are often run by religious groups.	☐	☐	☐
3. a. They feed any person who is hungry. b. Your religion is not important. c. When parentes say, "My child is hungry!" they are not ignored.	☐	☐	☐
4. a. The food Bank will feed those children. b. How do food banks get the food? c. Grocery stores donate good food they can't sell.	☐	☐	☐
5. a. The united states government sometimes gives surplus food. b. Churches and synagogues collect food. c. People make donations to fund the banks.	☐	☐	☐

Check your work on page 203.

POSSESSIVE NOUNS

> A noun that shows ownership is a *possessive noun.*

Singular possessive nouns always end in *'s*. Some examples of sentences with singular possessive nouns follow.

To show that Harold owns a jeep, you could write this sentence:

That is **Harold's** jeep.

What was added to the word *Harold* to show possession? _____

To show that Sis has a new silver purse, you could write this sentence:

Sis's new purse is silver.

What was added to the word *Sis* to show possession? _____

To show that one boy had a baby hamster, you could write this sentence:

The **boy's** hamster is a baby.

What was added to the word *boy* to show possession? _____

In all of those sentences, *'s* is added to the noun to show possession.

There are times when more than one person owns something. Then you must write ***plural possessive nouns***. When a plural noun ends in *s*, just add an apostrophe (') to make it possessive.

To show that two boys owned a baby hamster, you could write this sentence:

The **boys'** hamster is a baby.

What was added to the word *boys* to show possession? _____

To show that two ladies owned a boat, you could write:

The **ladies'** boat will be launched Tuesday.

What was added to the word *ladies* to show possession? _____

In both sentences, an apostrophe (') was added to show possession.

As you know, not all plural nouns end in *s*. If a plural noun does not end in *s*, add *'s* to show possession.

To show that several women have tennis racquets, you could write this sentence:

The **women's** racquets don't have strings yet.

What was added to the word *women* to show possession? _____

To show that several geese laid eggs, you could write this sentence:

The **geese's** eggs will hatch soon.

What was added to the word *geese* to show possession? _____

In both sentences, *'s* was added to show possession.

> ### Summary of Rules for Possessive Nouns
>
> 1. Add *'s* to a singular noun to make it possessive.
>   boss*'s* office—one boss has an office
>   child*'s* toy—one child has a toy
>
> 2. Add *'* to a plural noun ending in *s* to make it possessive.
>   bosses*'* offices—several bosses have offices
>
> 3. Add *'s* to a plural noun that does not end in *s* to make it possessive.
>   children*'s* toys—several children have toys

EXERCISE 6: WRITING POSSESSIVE NOUNS

Directions: Write the possessive form of the following nouns. The first two are done as examples.

1. coach: *coach's*

2. coaches: *coaches'*

3. army: _____

4. armies: _____

5. James: _____

6. woman: _____

7. women: _____

8. choir: _____

9. choirs: _____

10. Yim: _____

Check your work on page 203.

EXERCISE 7: MORE PRACTICE WITH POSSESSIVE NOUNS

Directions: Write the possessive form of the first noun in each pair of words. The first two have been done as examples.

1. cat cradle: *cat's cradle*

2. telephone ring: *telephone's ring*

3. busboys trays: _____

4. player helmet: _____

5. principal office: _____

6. Mickey house: _____

7. teachers meetings: _____

8. coach signals: _____

9. neighbors anniversary: _____

10. mechanic wrench: _____

Check your work on page 203.

PUTTING YOUR SKILLS TO WORK

Directions: This exercise will go in your writing folder or notebook. You will practice forming possessive, plural, and proper nouns. According to the following instructions, write five sentences. Be sure to write correctly, practicing the skills you have been learning throughout this book.

In the first sentence, use the possessive form of *Dracula.*
In the second sentence, use the possessive form of *sheep.*
In the third sentence, use the plural form of *city.*
In the fourth sentence, use the plural form of *woman.*
In the fifth sentence, use a proper noun with *Detective.*

☑ Writing Checklist

❏ Did you use the correct form of each of the five nouns?
❏ Are all proper nouns and first words of sentences capitalized?

PRONOUNS

As you learned before, pronouns take the place of nouns. They are used like nouns. They stand for the names of people, places, things, and ideas. Here are some sample sentences showing how pronouns take the place of nouns.

Gina is an experienced welder.
She is an experienced welder.

What pronoun took the place of *Gina* in the second sentence? _____

You were correct if you wrote *She.* Try another example.

The evening sky was covered with clouds.
The evening sky was covered with them.

What pronoun took the place of *clouds* in the second sentence? _____

If you answered *them*, you were correct. Now try one more example.

Frank's party lasted only ten minutes.
His party lasted only ten minutes.

What pronoun took the place of *Frank's* in the second sentence? _____

You were right if you wrote *His*.

Subject pronouns take the place of the subject of a sentence (like *She* in the sentence *She is an experienced welder.*). *Object pronouns* take the place of nouns that are not the subject of a sentence (like *them* in the example above). *Possessive pronouns* take the place of possessive nouns (like *his* in the example above). In the following chart are the pronouns you will be studying in this chapter.

Pronouns			
Subject	Object	Possessive Used with a noun	Used alone
I	me	my	mine
you	you	your	yours
he	him	his	his
she	her	her	hers
it	it	its	its
we	us	our	ours
they	them	their	theirs

SUBJECT PRONOUNS

Subject pronouns are used as the subject of a sentence. You should remember from Chapter 2 that the subject is the person, place, thing, or idea talked about in a sentence. Every sentence tells what the subject is or does.

The subject pronouns are *I, you, he, she, it, we*, and *they*. Here are some examples of how subject pronouns are used.

Adolph said not to listen to the radio.
He said not to listen to the radio.

Adolph is the subject of the sentence, so the pronoun *He* replaces *Adolph*.

The statements are not true.
They are not true.

The statements is the subject. The plural subject pronoun *They* replaces *The statements*.

Wendell and I will be careful.
We will be careful.

Wendell and I is the subject. The subject pronoun *We* replaces *Wendell and I*.

EXERCISE 8: USING SUBJECT PRONOUNS

Directions: On the blanks following these sentences, write the subject pronoun you could use to replace the underlined noun. The subject pronouns are *I, you, he, she, it, we,* and *they*. The first one is done as an example.

1. <u>Linda</u> encouraged her husband Paul to apply for a credit card. *she*

2. <u>Paul</u> seemed qualified for a card. _____

3. <u>Paul</u> had an excellent credit record, and his job was steady. _____

4. <u>Paul and Linda</u> were surprised by the company's response. _____

5. <u>The letter</u> said that Paul's salary was too low. _____

Check your work on page 203.

OBJECT PRONOUNS

Object pronouns are used whenever a pronoun is not the subject and does not show possession. The object pronouns are *me, you, him, her, it, us,* and *them*. Look in the chart on page 56 to see which object pronouns are different from the subject pronouns and which are the same.

Here are some sentences using object pronouns. The object pronoun is in dark type in each of the sentences.

Luis gave Ellen a birthday present.
Luis gave **her** a birthday present.

Luis is the subject. Since *Ellen* is not the subject, the object pronoun *her* replaces *Ellen*. Now look at another example.

After school, the bus took Artemas and Titus home.
After school, the bus took **them** home.

In this sentence, *the bus* is the subject. Since *Artemas and Titus* is not the subject, the object pronoun *them* is used.
What pronoun would you use in this sentence? Write it in the blank.

The rosebush gave Arthur great pleasure.

The rosebush gave _____ great pleasure.

You were correct if you wrote *him.* The subject is *The rosebush,* so *Arthur* cannot be the subject. Therefore, *Arthur* must be replaced by the object pronoun *him.*

EXERCISE 9: USING OBJECT PRONOUNS

Directions: In the blanks following these sentences, write the object pronoun you could use to replace the underlined noun. The object pronouns are *me, you, him, her, it, us,* and *them.* The first one is done as an example.

1. For the third time in two months, Bob glared at <u>the washing machine</u>.
   _*it*_

2. He wrote down the exact dates of each breakdown and handed the list to <u>his landlady</u>. _____

3. Mrs. Perry thanked <u>Bob</u> and promised to speak with the repairman.
   _____

4. When the machine stayed broken for another week, Bob sent letters to <u>Mrs. Perry and the repair company</u>. _____

5. "I pay my rent on time," wrote Bob. "This situation is unfair to <u>me and the other tenants</u>." _____

6. Bob received a call from <u>Mrs. Perry</u> two days later. _____

7. She told Bob that <u>the machine</u> was working again. _____

8. Everyone in Bob's building thanked <u>Bob</u> for getting the job done.
   _____

Check your work on page 203.

POSSESSIVE PRONOUNS

Possessive pronouns have the same purpose as possessive nouns: they show ownership. Look back at the chart on page 56 and read over the two columns of possessive pronouns. Notice that, unlike possessive nouns, none of the possessive pronouns contain an apostrophe (').

Some possessive pronouns appear with a noun to show who owns the noun. Those possessive pronouns are *my, your, his, her, its, our,* and *their.* Here are some examples of how this first group of possessive pronouns replaces possessive nouns.

> That is Harold's jeep.
> That is **his** jeep.

In that sentence, *his* replaces *Harold's* and appears with *jeep* to show who owns the jeep.

> The boys' hamster is a baby.
> **Their** hamster is a baby.

In that sentence, *Their* replaces *The boys'* and appears with *hamster* to show who owns the hamster.

The second group of possessive pronouns can stand alone. These pronouns are *mine, yours, his, hers, its, ours,* and *theirs.* Here are some examples of how these pronouns appear in sentences.

> The jeep is Harold's.
> The jeep is **his**.

> The baby hamster is the boys'.
> The baby hamster is **theirs**.

In those sentences, the possessive pronouns *his* and *theirs* replace the possessive nouns *Harold's* and *boys'*.

EXERCISE 10: USING POSSESSIVE PRONOUNS

Directions: In the blank following each sentence, write the possessive pronoun that can replace the underlined nouns. The first one is done as an example.

1. Have you seen <u>the Garcias'</u> new day care center? ____*their*____

2. They bought it last June with <u>Mr. Garcia's</u> savings. _____

3. One reason for <u>the center's</u> popularity is that it's just two blocks from the subway. _____

4. Also, parents value Mrs. Garcia's teaching experience and <u>Mrs. Garcia's</u> love of children. _____

5. The parents like to help out, so many ideas for games are <u>the parents'</u>. _____

6. Every time Lizzy leaves the center, she tries to take a doll or car that isn't <u>Lizzy's</u>. _____

7. So the Garcias spend time sorting <u>the children's</u> belongings. _____

8. Despite the confusion, Mrs. Garcia often thinks, "This place is really <u>mine and my husband's</u>."_____

Check your work on page 204.

EXERCISE 11: USING PRONOUNS

Directions: Underline the correct pronouns in the following paragraphs. You will be using subject, object, and possessive pronouns. The first one is done as an example.

Karen enjoys (<u>*her*</u>, *hers*) job at the Adult Learning Center. (*She, Her*) is the staff support specialist. She helps Larry with (*he, his*) teaching. Carol teaches there too and is well liked by (*she's, her*) students. The students look forward to coming to (*their, them*) classes.

The directors of the center are Vicki and George. (*They, Them*) count on government grants to fund the center's programs. (*Their, Theirs*) assistant, Bob, helps (*they, them*) get funding for the programs. (*He, Him*) is a very important member of the staff. All the Adult Learning Center staff members are quick to state, "(*We, Us*) believe in adult education!"

Check your work on page 204.

PRONOUN AGREEMENT

As you have been learning, to replace a noun with a pronoun you must figure out whether the noun is subject, object, or possessive. You must know what noun a pronoun is replacing to know what pronoun to use. Is the noun male, female, or neither? Is it singular or plural?

If a female's name is used, you must use *she, her,* or *hers.*

> **Eleanor Roosevelt** never went to grade school. But **she** became a world leader. The world respects **her** contributions to society.

Male names must be replaced with *he, his,* or *him.*

> **Albert Einstein** failed math as a child. However, **his** theory of relativity changed the world of science.

The names of animals, places, things, or ideas must be replaced with *it* or *its.*

> **The United Nations** is in New York City. **It** is a worldwide organization. One of **its** main interests is the children of the world.

Always use a singular pronoun to replace a singular noun and a plural pronoun to replace a plural noun.

> That **book** is interesting. You should read **it.**
> Those **books** are interesting. You should read **them.**

The first example talked about one book, so the pronoun *it* was used to replace the singular noun. The second example talked about more than one book, so the pronoun *them* was used to replace the plural noun.

EXERCISE 12: PRONOUN AGREEMENT

Directions: Fill in each blank with the appropriate pronoun. The word that the pronoun must agree with is in dark type. The first one is done as an example.

1. **Will Rogers** hated school and caused extensive damage to school property. In later years, ___*he*___ became a famous humorist.

2. **Jane Duncan** dropped out of school at the age of ten. _____ claimed to be sixteen.

3. **Beethoven** was deaf. Although he could not hear _____ music, the world still appreciates it.

4. These **rocks** will make a pretty garden border. I will put _____ around the edges.

5. The **dogs** may dig up the garden. _____ run through the yard all the time.

6. These **flowers** were planted last month. I can see _____ leaves coming up now.

7. This **plant** is growing fast. Soon _____ will have blossoms.

8. **Horace and I** have worked hard in the garden. _____ efforts will make this house more beautiful.

Check your work on page 204.

Complete the Following

Subject pronouns take the place of the _____ of a sentence.

Object pronouns take the place of _____ that are not the _____ of a sentence.

Possessive pronouns take the place of nouns that show _____ .

It is important to use a singular pronoun to replace a _____ _____ and a plural pronoun to replace a _____ _____ .

 PUNCTUATING PERFECTLY

APOSTROPHES IN CONTRACTIONS

Look at the two sentences below. How are they different?

She is a good person.
She's a good person.

In the second sentence, there is a contraction: *She's*. A contraction is formed when two words are combined into one word. An apostrophe (') shows where one or more letters have been left out and two words joined. In the example above, the two words *She is* become one word: *She's*. The letter *i* is dropped from the word *is*, and an apostrophe replaces it.

To make a contraction, replace the missing letter or letters with an apostrophe. Study the examples below and then complete the list.

I am   _I'm_

you are   _you're_

she is   _____

we will   _____   (*Hint:* Remove two letters from *will.*)

they are   _____

he is   _____

it is   _____

The correct contractions are *she's, we'll, they're, he's,* and *it's.*

Negatives are formed the same way.

did not   _didn't_

was not   _wasn't_

are not   _____

is not   _____

would not   _____

had not   _____

The correct contractions are *aren't, isn't, wouldn't,* and *hadn't.*

EXERCISE 13: FORMING CONTRACTIONS

Directions: Finish the following list of contractions. Two examples have been completed for you.

1. they have _they've_
2. does not _doesn't_
3. he is _____
4. I am _____
5. we are _____

6. is not _____
7. should not _____
8. they will _____
9. would not _____
10. that is _____

Check your work on page 204.

Contractions and Possessive Pronouns

You've probably noticed that apostrophes are used in both contractions and possessive nouns. However, apostrophes are *never* used in possessive pronouns. Be careful not to confuse possessive pronouns with contractions. If you can't tell which to use, substitute the two words the contraction stands for in the sentence to see if they make sense.

Here's an example. Which word correctly completes the sentence?

(Its, It's) cold outside.

As you know, *It's* is a contraction of *It is.* Try substituting *It is* in the sentence. Does the following sentence make sense?

It is cold outside.

Yes. If you can write *It is*, you can also write the contraction *It's*: It's cold outside.

Now look at another example. Which word is correct?

That dog is hurt. Something is wrong with *(its, it's)* paw.

Try substituting the words *it is* in the sentence. Does the following sentence make sense?

Something is wrong with it is paw.

No. That sentence doesn't make sense. So the correct word to complete the sentence must be the possessive pronoun *its.*

Something is wrong with its paw.

EXERCISE 14: CONTRACTIONS AND POSSESSIVE PRONOUNS

Directions: There are eight errors in the paragraph below. All of the mistakes have to do with contractions and possessives. Find each mistake, cross it out, and write the correct word above it. The first error is corrected for you.

It's
~~Its~~ always a good idea to decorate you're home. Even

people who don't have much spare time can hang pictures on

they're walls and put up curtains. Of course, its harder if your

working full-time. Gary, a friend of mine, did a nice job on he's apartment. I hope that he and his friend Pete will help me

out. Their really talented at decorating.

Check your work on page 204.

EXERCISE 15: CHAPTER REVIEW
Part 1
To complete this part of the review, use the information you studied in this chapter.

Directions: In this exercise, you will read three ways of writing each sentence. Choose the *correct* sentence by marking choice **a**, **b**, or **c**.

	a	b	c

1. **a.** Many United states citizens do not want nuclear power.
   b. Many united states citizens do not want nuclear power.
   c. Many United States citizens do not want nuclear power.

2. **a.** They say the accident at Three Mile Island showed how dangerous it can be.
   b. They say the accident at Three Mile island showed how dangerous it can be.
   c. They say the accident at three mile island showed how dangerous it can be.

3. **a.** Some children became sick after the accident.
   b. Some childrens became sick after the accident.
   c. Some childs became sick after the accident.

4. **a.** The residents of Harrisburg live close to the power plant.
   b. The Residents of Harrisburg live close to the power plant.
   c. The residents of harrisburg live close to the power plant.

5. **a.** The residents homes were in danger during the accident.
   b. The resident's home's were in danger during the accident.
   c. The residents' homes were in danger during he accident.

                                                     a   b   c

6. **a.** Some of these citizen's are leading the fight to   ☐   ☐   ☐
         close all nuclear power plants.
   b. Some of these citizens are leading the fight to
         close all nuclear power plants.
   c. Some of these Citizens are leading the fight
         to close all nuclear power plants.

Directions: In each of the following sentences, one or more nouns are incorrect. On the line under the sentence, write the sentence correctly.

7. Years ago, I went to hear senator Stevenson speak.

   _____

8. My Aunt always said he was her favorite Senator.

   _____

9. The year stevenson ran for president, dad bought a new ford.

   _____

Directions: Below is a list of pronouns to use in the exercise that follows. Fill each blank in the following sentences with one of the pronouns from the list. You should use each pronoun once.

       I   they   his   ours   hers   us   she   my

10. After the game, _____ drove my car home.

11. The man gave _____ paycheck to Housing for Humanity.

12. _____ brought her pets to the rabies clinic.

13. Suzette claimed that the purse was _____.

14. "Throw the Frisbee to _____!" screamed Pablo and Paco.

15. We went to visit the Archers, but _____ weren't home.

16. "Please give me _____ change," requested the diner.

17. "The car that was stolen was _____," cried Betty and Jerry.

Part 2

To complete this part of the review, use the information you studied in Chapter 2 about complete sentences, punctuation, and finding the subject of a sentence.

Directions: On the line under each exercise, write the sentence correctly. You may have to add words to make a complete sentence.

1. After the party, Dean.

   _____

2. everyone went to a local restaurant for dinner.

   _____

3. Look out—it's a raid?

   _____

4. stay in your seats.

   _____

5. Will be arrested.

   _____

Directions: Write the subject of each sentence in the blank. The first one is done as an example.

6. Did you find the album? _____*you*_____

7. Music always cheers me up. _____

8. Turn on the radio. _____

9. That DJ has a great voice. _____

10. In a few minutes, the news will come on. _____

11. Does Ilena like this song? _____

Check your work on pages 204–205.

YOUR TURN TO WRITE
A ONE-SIDED ARGUMENT

In your writing folder or notebook, you are going to share your opinion about something. Below are three possible topics.

1. People over twenty-one should not live with their parents.
2. Parents should have their kids arrested for illegal actions.
3. Drunk drivers should have to serve time in jail.

WRITING ASSIGNMENT

Directions: Choose one of the topics above (or think of another topic) and state your opinion. Imagine that you are having an argument with someone on the given topic. You know that there are good points and bad points for everything, but to win this argument you'll want to present points that support only the side of the issue that you chose.

Pick your topic and start writing. Write clearly and correctly, using the skills you have been practicing in this book.

☑ Writing Checklist

❑ Does every sentence you wrote support your opinion?
❑ Do all of your pronouns agree with the nouns they replace?
❑ Are your nouns used correctly?

CHAPTER 4

# JOURNAL WRITING
AN IMPORTANT PERSON

In this journal entry, try writing an "I just want to tell you how wonderful you are" letter. You now have an opportunity to say how much you appreciate someone. You can probably think of people who have had a positive effect on your life. You may not have ever let them know how much they helped you. If you want to, use your journal to write to at least one person who is important to you.

JOURNAL ENTRY

Directions: Has someone helped you to earn extra money? to lose weight? to become emotionally or physically stronger? Is there someone who has helped you with your schoolwork? Has your religious leader given a sermon that changed your life? Is there a teacher whom you really admire who had a positive influence on your life?

Have you ever thought, Someday, I'm going to tell that person just how much I appreciate him? Well, this is your chance.

Just write "Dear . . ." and continue writing. Get out that journal, choose your topic, and have fun! Remember, your journal is just for you. You don't have to worry about correct grammar and spelling.

LANGUAGE SKILLS
VERBS: FORM AND TENSE

WHAT IS A VERB?

You have already learned some things about verbs in Chapters 1 and 2. You might remember this definition:

> A *verb* is a word that shows action or being.

A verb can be an *action word* like *run, jump, skip, drink,* or *dance.* It can also be a *linking word* (being word) like *is, am, was,* or *were.*

The following sentences contain verbs. Underline the words that show what a noun is or does.

> The traffic roared through the tunnel.
> Drivers honked horns at each other.
> In the tunnel, the light glowed eerily.
> Many drivers were impatient.
> Overhead, highway patrolmen watched the scene on
>   television.
> At the tunnel's exit, a motorcycle cop waited for speeders.

Did you underline *roared, honked, glowed, were, watched,* and *waited*? If so, you have a good understanding of verbs.

Below is a list of nouns. In the space next to each noun, write a verb that tells something that the noun does.

gorillas _____

husbands _____

wives _____

cars _____

teachers _____

friends _____

dogs _____

You might have written that dogs bark and teachers teach. Maybe you wrote that friends share. Any word is a correct answer as long as it is a verb.

VERBS TELL TIME

Verbs tell time. When you talk about what you do today, what you did yesterday, and what you will do in the future, you use **verb tenses**. You change verb tenses to show when events in your life take place.

Think about this very moment as now. A verb that tells what you do now is a **present-tense** verb.

Right now, I **walk** slowly.

Present-tense verbs also tell what you do on a regular basis.

I always **walk** slowly.

Yesterday took place before now. Anything that happened before now— it doesn't matter how long ago—is part of your past. A verb that tells what you did before is a **past-tense** verb.

Last week, I **walked** slowly.

You also plan to do things tomorrow and weeks, months, and years from now. Anything that happens after now will happen in the future. A verb that tells what you will do at some later time is a **future-tense** verb.

Next week, I **will walk** slowly.

Now fill in the blanks below with five verbs showing things you do every day. See if you can put them in the present tense.

Every day I ___*sleep*___ , _____ ,
_____ , _____ , and _____ .

There are things you did yesterday that you did not do today. In the blanks below, list verbs that show things you did yesterday that you did not do today. See if you can put them in the past tense.

Yesterday I ___*danced*___ , _____ ,
_____ , _____ , and _____ .

Now list verbs that show things that you did not do today but will do tomorrow. See if you can put them in the future tense.

Tomorrow I ___*will*___ ___*shop*___ , I _____ _____ ,
I _____ _____ , I _____ _____ , and I

_____ _____ .

RECOGNIZING THE BASE VERB

In the examples on page 71, you saw the verbs *walk, walked,* and *will walk.* Here they are again:

PRESENT: Right now, I walk slowly.
PAST: Last week, I walked slowly.
FUTURE: Next week, I will walk slowly.

In those examples, the present-tense verb *walk* is the base verb. The past tense is formed by adding an ending, *ed,* to the base verb. The future tense is formed by adding a helping verb, *will,* to the base verb.

> The main verb is called the *base verb.* Verb tenses are formed by adding endings or helping verbs to the base verb.

As you study verbs in the rest of this chapter, you'll be learning to use base verbs with endings and helping verbs to form different verb tenses correctly.

All verbs change to the future tense according to the same pattern. Some verbs, like *walk,* also change to the present and past tenses according to a regular pattern. These verbs are *regular verbs.* You'll study how to form regular verbs first. Later in the chapter, you'll study some *irregular verbs.* Irregular verbs don't follow the regular patterns for changing tenses.

PRESENT TENSE OF REGULAR VERBS

The present tense shows that something is happening right now. It is also used to show that something takes place regularly. To form the present tense, you use the base verb by itself or the base verb plus *s.*

The following box shows how the present tense of the base verb *walk* is formed for different subjects. Notice that *s* is added to the base verb for some of the subjects. An *s* is added to make the verb "agree" with those subjects.

Subject	Present Tense
I, you, we, they, and all plural nouns	walk (base verb alone)
he, she, it, and all singular nouns	walks (base verb + *s*)

In the following sentences, the verbs end in *s* because their subjects are *he, she, it,* or singular nouns:

> She **looks** great in her new coat.
> Roger **seems** happy enough.
> The wind **feels** cool.

In one of the following sentences, the verb should end in *s*. Complete the sentences by writing *dance* or *dances* in each blank.

> My grandparents _____ in a contest every year.

> My grandmother _____ very gracefully.

For the first sentence, the correct answer is *dance,* since *grandparents* is a plural noun. The correct answer for the second sentence is *dances,* since *grandmother* is a singular noun.

EXERCISE 1: CHOOSING PRESENT-TENSE VERBS

Directions: Circle the subject in each sentence. Then underline the correct verb form. The first one is done as an example.

1. (Americans) *(enjoy, enjoys)* changes.

2. They *(like, likes)* to see their country grow.

3. I *(love, loves)* being a citizen.

4. I *(find, finds)* that many people are willing to help me.

5. They *(welcome, welcomes)* me with a place to live.

6. This year, a church *(sponsors, sponsor)* me.

7. A school *(gives, give)* me English classes.

8. I *(learns, learn)* a new alphabet.

9. My parents still *(live, lives)* in another country.

10. We *(write, writes)* to each other every week.

Check your work on page 205.

PAST TENSE OF REGULAR VERBS

The past tense shows that something took place in the past. Have you noticed what endings are usually added to base verbs to show the past tense? Most regular verbs take an *ed* ending to form the past tense. Regular verbs that end in *e* have only the letter *d* added to form the past tense.

Here are some examples of how to form the past tense of regular verbs.

base verb + ending	= past tense
walk + ed	= walked
spell + ed	= spelled
change + d	= changed
love + d	= loved

Now see if you can write some past-tense verbs. The following paragraph has three blanks. Fill in the past tense of the base verb underneath each blank to complete the paragraph.

Two years ago, Al _____ exercise. Last year, he
                        (hate)

_____ one mile a day. Now Al walks three miles a day.
    (walk)

He looks physically fit. Two years ago, he _____ terrible.
                                            (look)

Now he hates to miss his daily exercise.

You should have written *hated, walked,* and *looked.* What letters did you add to the verbs to make them past tense? _____

FORMING THE FUTURE TENSE

The future tense shows that something will take place in the future. Verbs written in the future tense show that something has not happened yet. Here are three sentences using the future tense of the base verbs *fly, cry,* and *sigh.*

Maria **will fly** to Puerto Rico.
She **will cry** when she sees her family.
During her visit, Maria **will sigh** with happiness.

What helping verb comes before the base verbs *fly, cry,* and *sigh* to show the future tense? _____

The helping verb is *will.* You can now make up a rule about future-tense verbs. See if you can complete the following rule.

Complete the Following

To form the future tense of any verb, add the helping verb _____ in front of the verb.

EXERCISE 2: WRITING THE PAST AND FUTURE TENSES

Directions: Write the past and future tenses of the following base verbs. The first one is done for you as an example.

Base Verb	Past	Future
1. look	*looked*	*will look*
2. move	_____	_____
3. live	_____	_____
4. earn	_____	_____
5. save	_____	_____
6. play	_____	_____

Check your work on page 205.

IRREGULAR VERBS

In Exercise 2, you added an *ed* to put each of those verbs in the past tense. But be careful! Not all verbs change to the past tense according to the regular pattern. There are many irregular verbs, mostly in the past tense.

There is only one way to get to know irregular verbs. You must study them until you can remember them. Actually, you probably know the correct past-tense forms of many irregular verbs right now. Here is an exercise that will let you find out if you know the past tense of some common irregular verbs.

EXERCISE 3: PAST TENSE OF IRREGULAR VERBS

Directions: Fill in the past tense of as many verbs as you can. Don't worry if you don't know them all. If you know half of the answers, you are doing excellent work. When you have filled in as many as you know, turn to the answer key, check your work, and fill in the rest. The first two are done for you as examples.

Base Verb

Past Tense

1. give   I ____*gave*____ last month.

2. tell   I ____*told*____ him yesterday.

3. run   I _____ a mile yesterday.

4. become   I _____ a senior lifesaver last year.

5. see   I _____ him the day before he left.

6. take   I _____ the test some time ago.

7. teach   I _____ two days ago.

8. come   I _____ last week.

9. read   I _____ the paper last Sunday.

10. bring   I _____ it some time ago.

11. say   I _____ so yesterday.

12. make   I _____ the cake last night.

13. go   I _____ home yesterday.

14. sit   I _____ there the night before last.

15. do   I _____ it a minute ago.

16. have   I _____ the book last night.

17. sell   I _____ the car four months ago.

18. drink   I _____ milk this morning.

19. write   I _____ a letter yesterday.

20. eat   I _____ the cake last night.

Check your work on page 205.

AVOIDING ERRORS WITH IRREGULAR VERBS

In Exercise 3, you filled in the blanks with the past-tense forms of many irregular verbs. None of these forms needed helping verbs. There are some other past tenses that do require helping verbs, but you will not be studying all of those tenses in this book. However, some very common mistakes are made when people confuse the different past tenses. Right now you'll learn to avoid some of those mistakes.

Study the following pair of sentences. The correct sentence uses the form of the past you learned in Exercise 3. It does not require a helping verb. The other sentence contains a mistake because it uses a form that cannot stand alone.

CORRECT: I did my homework already.

MISTAKE: I done my homework already.

The correct past tense of *do* is *did*. The word *done* is used to form a tense that requires a helping verb, so *done* is never correct when it is used alone.

Here are some other similar pairs of sentences. Study each pair to be sure you know which past-tense form can be used without a helping verb.

CORRECT: She went home yesterday.

MISTAKE: She gone home yesterday.

CORRECT: We came home last night.

MISTAKE: We come home last night.

CORRECT: I ran a mile last week.

MISTAKE: I run a mile last week.

CORRECT: Eli saw a bird over there.

MISTAKE: Eli seen a bird over there.

CORRECT: Jesse was helping me.

MISTAKE: Jesse been helping me.

**EXERCISE 4: CHOOSING THE CORRECT
PAST-TENSE FORM**

Directions: Underline the correct verb to complete each of the following sentences. The first one is done as an example.

1. Angie (*seen, saw*) a prowler in the parking lot.

2. Last night the Olshers (*ran, run*) into the Millers.

3. Horace (*was, been*) in that bowling league for years.

4. Denise (*done, did*) the milking at dawn.

5. Ross (*come, came*) to the office at 3:00 A.M.

6. We (*went, gone*) camping for our vacation.

Check your work on page 205.

Complete the Following

What is a verb? _____

_____

What three verb tenses have you learned so far? _____

_____

IMPORTANT IRREGULAR VERBS

On the next few pages, you will be studying three very important irregular verbs. These verbs are used so much that writers must know them in order to write correctly.

The Base Verb *Be*

As you already know, the most common linking verbs are forms of *be*. In fact, forms of *be* are some of the most frequently used verbs.

The verb *be* is very irregular because its forms change for different subjects in both the present tense and the past tense. The forms of the three tenses for *be* are in the following chart. Study and learn them all.

Subject	Present	Past	Future
I	am	was	will be
he, she, it and all singular nouns	is		
you, we, they, and all plural nouns	are	were	

Now try a few examples. Choose the correct form of *be* to complete the following sentences.

I *(be, am)* furious with those boys.

Tom *(was, were)* about to put his brother in the washing machine.

You *(is, are)* kidding!

They *(was, were)* both giggling.

In the first sentence, *am* agrees with *I*. In the second sentence, *was* agrees with the singular noun *Tom*. In the third sentence, *are* agrees with *You*. In the fourth sentence, *were* agrees with *They*.

EXERCISE 5: FORMS OF *BE*

Directions: Underline the correct verb in the following sentences. The first one is done as an example.

1. They *(was, _were_)* planning to get married.

2. You *(is, are)* going to take bus number five.

3. Erika *(was, were)* angry about the robbery.

4. The station wagon *(is, are)* ready for the junkyard.

5. The doctor *(are, is)* fond of his elderly patients.

6. We *(was, were)* going to be friends forever.

7. Ms. Gallagher *(is, are)* concerned about her frequent headaches.

8. My parents (*is, are*) not sure that they want a divorce.

9. I (*was, were*) thrilled with the news.

10. Your building (*was, were*) infested with termites.

Check your work on page 205.

The Base Verbs *Have* and *Do*

There are a few other confusing irregular verbs that we need to use every day. Two of the most common ones are *have* and *do*.

You may already know how to use these verbs correctly most of the time. Try to correct the paragraph below to see how much you already know about those two verbs. Draw a line through each verb you think is incorrect and write the correct form above it. There is one mistake in each sentence.

> My brother have to quit his job. His wife don't like it when he leaves home at 5 A.M. to go to work. She have to understand that he will get fired if he comes to work late. My brother's children does not understand him either. They has no time to see him.

After you've made all the changes you think are necessary, read the corrected paragraph below.

> My brother **has** to quit his job. His wife **doesn't** like it when he leaves home at 5 A.M. to go to work. She **has** to understand that he will get fired if he comes to work late. My brother's children **do** not understand him either. They **have** no time to see him.

How did you do? Are you surprised at how much you know about these verbs? If you got the exercise completely correct, the next few exercises will probably not be very hard for you. If you made a few mistakes, take the time to study carefully the forms of *have* and *do*.

Forms of *Have*

The following chart shows the forms of all three tenses of the irregular verb *have*.

Subject	Present	Past	Future
I, you, we, they, and all plural nouns	have	had	will have
he, she, it and all singular nouns	has		

When you are deciding which form of *have* to use, remember that the present tense is either *has* or *have* and the past tense is always *had*. The future is always *will have*.

EXERCISE 6: FORMS OF *HAVE*

Directions: Complete the following sentences using the correct form and tense of the verb *have*. The first one is done as an example.

1. Tom ___*has*___ a good job.
   (present)

2. He _____ time to go to the movies each weekend.
   (present)

3. He _____ fun at the movies next weekend.
   (future)

4. After work on Friday, he remembered that he _____ to use an automated teller machine to make *(past)* a withdrawal.

5. When he found an ATM, he realized he _____ forgotten his personal identification number (PIN).
   (past)

6. Tom groaned, "Now I _____ to go home and find my PIN."
   (present)

7. If Tom can't find his number, he _____ to contact the bank.
   (future)

Check your work on page 205.

Forms of *Do*

The following chart shows the present-, past-, and future-tense forms of the irregular verb *do*.

Subject	Present	Past	Future
I, you, we, they, and all plural nouns	do	did	will do
he, she, it and all singular nouns	does		

When you are deciding which form of *do* to use, remember that the present tense is either *do* or *does* and the past tense is always *did*. The future tense is always *will do*.

EXERCISE 7: FORMS OF *DO*

Directions: Complete the following sentences using the correct form of the verb *do*. The first one is done as an example.

1. __*Do*__ you have a monthly household budget?
    (present)

2. Most people _____ not bother to make a budget.
    (present)

3. If they _____, they might be surprised by where their money goes.
    (past)

4. My family _____ a budget last month, and we were shocked.
    (past)

5. My brother _____ not realize how much money he spends on clothes. *(present)*

6. Next month, he _____ without any new clothes.
    (future)

7. My sister _____ not need any more new clothes either.
    (present)

8. In the future, we all _____ without videotapes.
    (future)

9. I _____ not realize that I was paying for the video store owner's
    (past)
    new car.

10. In the future we _____ a budget each month.
    (future)

Check your work on page 205.

TIME CLUES TO VERB TENSES

Often you will be able to decide what verb tense (past, present, or future) to use by clue words in a sentence.

Words like *now, this minute,* and *today* tell you that the sentence takes place in the present.

Right this minute, I love you.

That sentence is written in the _____ tense. The clue words that

let you know are _____ _____ _____.

Words like *yesterday, last year, some time ago,* and *before* tell you that the sentence takes place in the past.

Last year, I loved you.

That sentence is written in the _____ tense. The clue words in

the sentence are _____ _____.

Words like *tomorrow, in three hours,* and *next year* tell you that the sentence takes place in the future.

Next year, I will love you.

That sentence is written in the _____ tense. The clue words that

tell you that the action will take place in the future are_____ _____.

EXERCISE 8: USING TIME CLUES

Directions: Write the correct form of the base verb to complete each sentence. Underline the time clue in each sentence that tells you what tense to choose. The first one is done as an example.

1. *(want)* <u>Today</u> many people ____*want*____ to lose weight.

2. *(work)* Last year Rob _____ out to tone up his muscles.

3. *(wake)* Now we _____ up early every day.

4. *(go)* Tomorrow Anne _____ to her aerobics class.

5. *(buy)* These days, Americans _____ a lot of diet soft drinks.

6. *(run)* Next week Liz _____ fifty miles.

7. *(exercise)* Last week Liz _____ so much that she got sick.

Check your work on page 206.

PUTTING YOUR SKILLS TO WORK

Directions: Use the information in this chapter to complete the following assignment. Write carefully and correctly, paying special attention to the verbs. Add this assignment to the others in your writing folder or notebook. Don't forget to date your entry.

   Look at the picture. Imagine you are one of the people in the picture. Write a paragraph in your notebook that tells what happened before the scene in the picture (past), what is happening in the picture (present), and what will happen next (future).

   Try to use at least two sentences in the past tense, two sentences in the present tense, and two sentences in the future tense.

   If you have trouble getting started, you can use this sentence as your first sentence.

   Matthew's letter said he was coming home on Tuesday.

☑ Writing Checklist

❑ Do you have two sentences written in the past tense?
❑ Do you have two sentences written in the present tense?
❑ Do you have two sentences written in the future tense?
❑ Are your verb forms correct?

THE CONTINUING TENSES
Another Way to Form the Present

You have already learned to form the present tense by using the base verb or the base verb plus *s* or *es*. Another present tense, the **present continuing tense**, shows that an action is continuing in the present. The present continuing tense is formed by using *am, is*, or *are* as a helping verb with the base verb plus *ing*.

This sentence uses the present continuing tense.

The clown **is laughing**.

There are two words in the verb of that sentence: *is laughing*. The helping verb is *is*. The base verb is *laugh*. The ending *ing* is added to *laugh*.

Can you pick out the present-continuing-tense verbs in the next two examples? Underline the verbs.

The workers are striking.
I am walking the picket line.

Did you underline *are striking* and *am walking*? They are the verbs in those sentences.

You can add *ing* to any base verb. On the line below, combine the verbs *swear, think*, and *choose* with the *ing* ending. (If a base verb ends in *e*, drop the *e* before adding *ing*.)

_____

You should have written *swearing, thinking*, and *choosing*.

Now write the three helping verbs that can be used before the base verb plus *ing* to form the present continuing tense: _____, _____, and _____.

You have already studied how to make *am, is*, and *are* agree with different subjects. You can review that information in the following chart, which shows all the present continuing forms of the verb *walk*.

Subject	Helping Verb	Base Verb + *ing*
I	am	
you, we, they, and all plural nouns	are	walking
he, she, it and all singular nouns	is	

EXERCISE 9: THE PRESENT CONTINUING TENSE

Directions: Complete each sentence by underlining the correct verb. Make sure that the verb you choose agrees with the subject. The first one is done for you as an example.

1. In my class, everyone *(is studying, are studying)* for an important test.

2. We *(be working, are working)* at different speeds and are good at different things.

3. Anna *(is learning, are learning)* fractions faster than Dave or I.

4. Some students *(is writing, are writing)* sentences with no trouble.

5. My science class *(is changing, are changing)* what we do every day.

6. Maria *(is helping, be helping)* me with my math.

7. The teacher *(is communicating, are communicating)* with his class better than he used to.

8. I *(is enjoying, am enjoying)* my math class this year because I understand it.

Check your work on page 206.

Another Way to Form the Past

Compare the two sentences below. How are they alike? How are they different?

> Rafael is running.
> Rafael was running.

The verb in the first sentence is *is running*. That verb is in the present continuing tense. The action is taking place now.

Look at the second sentence. It also uses the word *running*, but the helping verb is *was*. As you know, *was* is a past-tense verb. So that verb is in the **past continuing tense**, which shows that an action was continuing in the past.

The chart on the next page shows how to form the past continuing tense of the verb *walk* for different subjects.

Subject	Helping Verb	Base Verb + *ing*
you, we, they, and all plural nouns	were	walking
he, she, it and all singular nouns	was	

Now you try writing some verbs in the past continuing tense. Complete the following sentences by filling in the correct past continuing form of the base verb.

It _____*was raining*_____ hard that day.
      (rain)

Caren _____ when she said that.
      (joke)

The children _____ when we got home.
      (sleep)

You should have written *was joking* in the second sentence because *Caren* is a singular noun. In the third sentence, *were sleeping* agrees with the plural noun *children*.

EXERCISE 10: THE PAST CONTINUING TENSE

Directions: Complete each sentence below with the correct form of the past continuing tense. Remember, you need to use a helping verb, either *was* or *were*. The base verb must have an *ing* ending. Use the base verb below each blank. The first one is done as an example.

1. It _____*was raining*_____, and the streets were slippery as I drove
      (rain)
to work one morning.

2. I _____ too fast, and I hit two other cars.
      (drive)

3. The other drivers _____ when they got out of their cars.
      (smile)

4. "We _____ in for repairs anyway, so don't worry," they
said.   *(go)*

5. My boss _____ for me when I got to work.
      (look)

6. She said that she _____ me the day off and a big raise.
      (give)

7. Two twenty-dollar bills _____ along the sidewalk

(blow)

when I left, so I picked them up.

8. I _____ about going back to sleep as I drove home.

(think)

9. I _____ , and I couldn't wait to jump under my covers.

(yawn)

10. Suddenly my alarm clock _____.

(ring)

11. I _____!

(dream)

Check your work on page 206.

PUNCTUATING PERFECTLY

USING QUOTATION MARKS

Quotation marks (". . .") are used for a number of things. In this book you will learn the main use for quotation marks: to show direct quotes.

> ***Quotation marks*** are used to tell the reader that the words between them are exactly what someone said.

Here is an example:

"Don't do anything I wouldn't do," said Lee.

The words between the quotation marks are a direct quote. You know that Lee said these exact words: *Don't do anything I wouldn't do.* A direct quote repeats the exact words that someone used.

Here are two more examples of direct quotes:

"Our team won the championship," said Mike.
Mike said, "Our team won the championship."

Both of those sentences give you the same information. However, there are a few differences to notice.

In the first example, the direct quote comes first in the sentence. There is a comma (,) after the word *championship* and before the end quotation mark. The period comes after the last word in the sentence, *Mike*.

In the second sentence, the quote is at the end of the sentence. The comma (,) is after the word *said* and in front of the first quotation mark. The period is still at the end of the sentence, but it is inside the end quotation mark.

In the second sentence, the first word of the quote (*Our*) begins with a capital letter even though it is in the middle of the sentence. If a quote is a complete sentence, it always begins with a capital letter.

Here are a few more examples. Notice that the quote in the third sentence is a question, so a question mark comes before the end quotation mark.

> "I really have to get a new car," said Pedro.
> "My old car needs too many repairs," he complained.
> Estralita asked, "Why don't you clean it up and sell it?"
> She said, "It would be worth more money if it looked good."

Now you can practice adding quotation marks to sentences. The sentences below all contain direct quotes. Add quotation marks to show the quotes.

> It would take me forever to shine it up, said Pedro.
> I really need help with the job, he stated.
> Estralita asked, Would you pay me if I helped you?
> Then she added, If you drive me to work every day, I'll help you
>   for free.

Check the first sentence. Do you have quotation marks before the word *It* and after the comma? In the second sentence, you should have quotation marks before *I* and after the comma. In the third sentence, you should have quotation marks before *Would* and after the question mark. In the final sentence, do you have quotation marks before *If* and after the period? Make any necessary corrections to your work.

EXERCISE 11: USING QUOTATION MARKS

Directions: The following sentences form a conversation. Add quotation marks wherever they are needed.

1. I think the best years of a person's life are his teen years, said Raymond.

2. His mother laughed and said, That's because you are a teenager.

3. Actually, you will have more fun once you are an adult, said his twenty-two-year-old brother, John.

4. What will happen to me once I reach thirty? John wondered.

5. You'll be on your way to forty, and believe me, those are really the best years, said Mom.

6. Dad piped in, Oh, I don't know, I think I'm even better-looking at fifty.

7. John asked, How were the sixties, Grandma?

8. They were great, Grandma responded.

9. However, the seventies are the best, she said, smiling.

10. I can say whatever I want, do whatever I want, and go wherever I want—senior citizenship is sensational! Grandma exclaimed.

Check your work on page 206.

PUTTING YOUR SKILLS TO WORK

Now you have a chance to show that you know how to use quotation marks. In your writing folder or notebook, write a conversation between a man and a woman. You might want to have them talking about the first time that they met or about their family budget. Or you can think of another topic to have them talk about. Be sure to write carefully and correctly, using the skills you have studied in this book.

The conversation you write should have at least four sentences.

Sentence 1 should begin with *He said*.
Sentence 2 should begin with *She replied*.
Sentence 3 should end with *she added*.
Sentence 4 should end with *he replied*.

☑ Writing Checklist

❑ Do you have quotation marks at the beginning and end of direct quotes in all the sentences?
❑ Does the first word inside the quotation marks begin with a capital letter?
❑ Is there a comma before the beginning of the quotation in sentences 1 and 2?
❑ Is there a comma before the end quotation marks in sentences 3 and 4?

Complete the Following

A direct quote repeats _____.

_____ _____ are used to set off a direct quote.

Quotation marks look like this: _____

EXERCISE 12: CHAPTER REVIEW

Part 1

To complete this part of the review, you will use the information you have been studying in Chapter 4: verbs and verb tenses.

Directions: Complete the following.

1. Decide whether each verb in the following list is in the past, present, or future tense. Then put each word in the appropriate column of the chart below. The first three are done as examples.

   jump, sang, will find, looked, swim, flew, fall, danced, will write, claim, diagnosed, will examine, drive, will walk, saw, will want, had, are, was, will paint, drew, will say, talk, hopes, is

Past	Present	Future
sang	jump	will find

Directions: Read each sentence carefully. Three ways to write the underlined part of each sentence are given. Choose the way that makes the sentence correct. Choice *a* is always the same as the original underlined part.

	a	b	c

2. The community center <u>start</u> a gymnastics program for toddlers.   ☐ ☐ ☐
   a. start
   b. is starting
   c. be starting

3. That politician <u>were</u> guilty of discrimination.   ☐ ☐ ☐
   a. were
   b. are
   c. is

4. Our neighbors <u>are having</u> a huge argument.   ☐ ☐ ☐
   a. are having
   b. is having
   c. having

5. The circus <u>stop</u> here each year.   ☐ ☐ ☐
   a. stop
   b. will stops
   c. stops

6. Our cat <u>killed</u> three mice last month and brought them all home.   ☐ ☐ ☐
   a. killed
   b. is killing
   c. will kill

7. Two years ago, my father <u>decide</u> to go back to school.   ☐ ☐ ☐
   a. decide
   b. decided
   c. will decide

8. Todd <u>walk</u> six miles after his car broke down.   ☐ ☐ ☐
   a. walk
   b. walking
   c. walked

9. We <u>be</u> ready to leave for school now.   ☐ ☐ ☐
   a. be
   b. is
   c. are

	a	b	c

10. Theo <u>turn</u> the radio on as soon as he gets home from work.

    a. turn
    b. are turning
    c. turns

11. Velma <u>done</u> the copying three times last week.

    a. done
    b. did
    c. will do

Part 2

To complete this part of the review, you will have to use the information you studied in Chapters 2 and 3: possessives and contractions, complete sentences, pronouns, and common and proper nouns.

Directions: Each of the following sentences contains one error. Write each sentence correctly on the blank line. The first one is done as an example.

1. Her childrens room is a mess.

    Her children's room is a mess.

2. Some children keep their Rooms very neat and clean.

    _____

3. I cant blame her children for being messy.

    _____

4. Their just like her.

    _____

5. Doesn't like to clean her room either.

    _____

6. Them will all clean their rooms today.

    _____

Directions: Complete the following.

7. What is a fragment? _____

_____

8. A sentence has two parts: a _____ and a

_____ .

9. A proper noun always begins with a _____ _____ .

Check your work on page 206.

YOUR TURN TO WRITE
TELLING A STORY

It's time to take out your writing folder or notebook again. You will have a choice of two assignments. Write carefully and correctly, using all the skills you have been practicing in this book. Remember, you have to do only one of these assignments.

WRITING ASSIGNMENT

Choice 1

Directions: Think back to kindergarten or grade school. Do you remember a typical day in school: recess, your teachers, the kids . . . ? Everyone has special memories about that time in his or her life. Some people enjoyed that time in their lives, while others were miserable.

If you choose this assignment, it's time to tell your story. Write at least three paragraphs.

In the first paragraph, write about a typical day in grade school.

In the second paragraph, write about a typical day in your current school.

In the third paragraph, write about a typical school day you would like to have in the future.

Finally, you might want to write a fourth paragraph, sharing some information to tie the first three paragraphs together.

Choice 2

Directions: If you would prefer a different assignment, try writing a story. Include quotations from the people involved in the story. You might want to tell about meeting someone and falling in love at first sight. Or you might want to tell about a funny experience you had and what people said. The story doesn't have to be about you, and it doesn't have to be true. You're welcome to use your imagination! Whatever you decide, remember to use quotations from the people involved in the incident.

Take out that notebook, remember to date the entry, and start writing!

☑ *Writing Checklist*

❑ If you chose the first assignment, did you use a variety of tenses correctly? Were you able to explain yourself clearly?

❑ If you chose the second assignment, do you have quotation marks at the beginning and end of all the direct quotes?

C H A P T E R 5

JOURNAL WRITING
BRAINSTORMING

This journal entry will give you an opportunity to try a writing technique called *brainstorming*.

Brainstorming means writing all your thoughts about a topic. You write the thoughts down as quickly as possible and in whatever order they pop into your mind. Some of the thoughts may not seem to be a part of the topic. Don't worry about that. Just decide on a topic and write everything that comes to mind.

One thought will lead to another. You might even discover that you're thinking faster than you're writing. When you brainstorm, you don't need to write complete sentences or worry about correct spelling. Just jot down words and ideas until you are sure you don't have anything else to write. You may be surprised at the large number of ideas on the paper!

JOURNAL ENTRY

Directions: For this journal entry, brainstorm about one of these three topics or choose your own topic.

- What my perfect job would be like
- Being a teenager
- My pet

Brainstorming is part of a writing process. When you have finished brainstorming, you have many thoughts on paper. It's time to organize those thoughts and then turn them into one or more paragraphs about one topic. One easy way to organize a list of brainstormed ideas is to number them in the order you want to write about them. You might find that you don't want to use all the ideas you brainstormed. That's fine—it's your writing.

Here's an example of how one writer brainstormed on the topic "my pet." After she brainstormed, she put numbers next to the items in her brainstorm list to show the order in which she wanted to put them in her paragraph. She also crossed out some items.

My Pet

1 cat named Misty

~~canned cat food stinks~~

4 sleeps with me at night

6 yowls for food

3 doesn't like anyone but me

2 gray with white paws

~~neighbors have a cat too~~

5 had her kittens under my bed

After organizing her brainstorm list, the writer used it to write the following paragraph.

> My cat's name is Misty. She is very pretty, with gray fur and white paws. She doesn't like anyone but me, and she sleeps with me every night. When she had kittens, she hid under my bed to give birth. When she is hungry, she sits on the kitchen windowsill and yowls noisily for food. She can be a pest, but she is good company for me.

Now it's your turn. Get out your journal, pick your topic, and start brainstorming! When you have finished brainstorming, organize your brainstormed ideas and write at least one paragraph.

Remember, this is your journal, and it's just for you. You don't have to worry about grammar and spelling in your journal.

LANGUAGE SKILLS
SUBJECT-VERB AGREEMENT

Subject-verb agreement is making the verb in a sentence agree with the subject of that sentence. You practiced subject-verb agreement in Chapter 4 when you chose different forms of verbs for different subjects. Since subject-verb agreement is so important to good writing, you'll be studying it more carefully in this chapter.

Except for the irregular verb *be*, which you learned in Chapter 4, verbs change form for different subjects only in the present tense.

PRONOUNS AS SUBJECTS

In this section of Chapter 5, you will review how to make verbs agree with subject pronouns. Here are the subject pronouns with the correct present tense of the verb *swim*.

I
You   swim.
We
They

He
She   swims.
It

Which pronouns need a verb that ends in *s*? _____

Which pronouns need a verb that does not end in *s*? _____

_____

Rule for Subject-Verb Agreement with Pronouns

In the present tense, the verb must end in *s* if the subject is *he, she* or *it*. If the subject is *I, you, we,* or *they*, the verb does not end in *s*.

Try out the rule you just learned. Underline the correct verb to complete each of the following sentences.

They (*swim, swims*) at the beach every Saturday.

He (*laugh, laughs*) at all my jokes.

I (*look, looks*) great in my black leather jacket.

In the second sentence, *laughs* agrees with *He*. In the third sentence, *look* agrees with *I*.

Usually *s* is added to the end of a base verb for the subjects *he*, *she*, and *it*. However, when the base verb ends in a hissing sound (*s*, *x*, *z*, *sh*, or *ch*), *es* is added. In the following sentences, the base verbs have *es* added for subject-verb agreement.

> She **washes** the car on Sunday mornings.
> He **fixes** waffles for breakfast.
> It **fizzes** when you pour it.

EXERCISE 1: SUBJECT-VERB AGREEMENT WITH PRONOUNS

Directions: Underline the correct form of the verb to complete each sentence. Follow the rule for subject-verb agreement with pronouns. The first one is done as an example.

1. He *(own, owns)* a garage on 42nd Street.

2. We *(take, takes)* all our cars and trucks to his shop.

3. They *(come, comes)* back as good as new.

4. You *(get, gets)* your money's worth at that garage.

5. He *(fuss, fusses)* over every detail.

6. She *(thank, thanks)* him for taking good care of her car.

Check your work on page 206.

WHAT ABOUT IRREGULAR VERBS?

In Chapter 4, you learned the forms of three very important irregular verbs: *be, have,* and *do.* Right now, you'll review those three verbs to practice subject-verb agreement. You'll also learn the present tense of one new irregular verb: *go.*

Start by looking at just one irregular verb. Here are the subject pronouns with the correct present-tense forms of *have:*

Which pronouns need the form of the verb that ends in *s*? _____

Which pronouns need the form of the verb that does not end in *s*?

_____

Did you notice that the rule on page 98 still applies, even though *have* is an irregular verb? Go back to page 98 now and reread the rule. Notice that even though spellings are irregular, the forms for *he, she,* and *it* always end in *s.*

Now try applying the subject-verb agreement rule with irregular verbs. Underline the correct form of the verb to complete each of the following sentences. The first one is done for you as an example.

We (<u>do</u>, *does*) the dishes once a day.

She (*have, has*) the shopping list.

They (*are, is*) in the clothes hamper.

In the second sentence, *has* agrees with *She.* In the third sentence, *are* agrees with *They.*

Only one verb changes form for different subjects in the past tense. That verb is *be.* Look at the past-tense forms of *be* for different subjects.

I   was   he
                        she   ] was
you   it
we   ] were
they

Notice that in the past tense *I was* breaks the subject-verb agreement rule because the verb ends in *s*. This is the only exception to the rule.

Underline the correct past-tense form of *be* to complete the following sentences.

> I *(were, <u>was</u>)* happy to see you.
>
> It *(were, was)* done when I left.
>
> They *(were, was)* on the kitchen table.

You should have underlined *was* in the second sentence and *were* in the third sentence.

EXERCISE 2: SUBJECT-VERB AGREEMENT WITH IRREGULAR VERBS

Directions: Underline the correct form of the irregular verb to complete each sentence. Follow the subject-verb agreement rule and refer to the charts of irregular verb forms on pages 79–82 as much as necessary.

1. We *(am, is, are)* happy to see you.

2. They *(have, has)* dinner at 8:00 on most nights.

3. I *(am, are, is)* ready to sing now, Fred.

4. She *(do, does)* whatever her friends tell her.

5. He *(were, was)* on the phone when I arrived.

6. They *(do, does)* the laundry every weekend.

7. She *(have, has)* enough talent to get a part in the school play this year.

8. We *(do, does)* everything we can for you.

9. You *(were, was)* not invited to this party.

10. You *(am, are, is)* not old enough to drink.

Check your work on page 207.

SINGULAR AND PLURAL NOUNS AS SUBJECTS

The subject of a sentence can be either a subject pronoun, a singular noun, or a plural noun. Do you remember what *singular* and *plural* mean? Write the definitions below.

SINGULAR: _____

PLURAL: _____

Singular means "one." When a noun is singular, it refers to only one person, place, thing, or idea. *Plural* means "more than one." When a noun is plural, it refers to more than one person, place, thing, or idea.

You have already learned how to make verbs agree with all the subject pronouns. Now you can easily learn how to make verbs agree with singular subjects and plural subjects.

A singular subject can always be replaced by *he, she*, or *it*. Therefore, a verb must end in *s* to agree with a singular noun. Cross out the subject of the following sentence and replace it with *he, she,* or *it*. Then underline the correct verb.

The alligator (*swim, swims*) slowly through the swamp.

In that sentence, *alligator* is the singular subject. *The alligator* can be replaced by *It*. Therefore, the verb must end in *s*. Here is the correct answer:

       It
~~The alligator~~ (*swim, <u>swims</u>*) slowly through the swamp.

Now try another example. Cross out the subject of the following sentence and replace it with *he, she,* or *it*. Then underline the correct verb.

Samantha (*are, is*) a busy photographer.

In that sentence, *Samantha* is the singular subject. *Samantha* can be replaced by *She*. The verb must end in *s* to agree with *She*, so the correct verb is *is*.

A plural subject can always be replaced by *they*, so a verb must not end in *s* to agree with a plural subject. Cross out the plural subject of the following sentence and replace it with *they*. Then underline the correct verb.

The women (*laugh, laughs*) loudly.

In that sentence, women is the plural subject. *The women* can be replaced by *They*. The verb must not end in *s* to agree with *They*, so the correct verb is *laugh*.

Here is the subject-verb agreement rule again. Now it includes singular and plural nouns as subjects in addition to subject pronouns.

> ### Subject-Verb Agreement Rule
>
> In the present tense, the verb must end in *s* if the subject is *he, she, it,* or a singular noun. If the subject is *I, you, we, they,* or a plural noun, the verb does not end in *s.*

Countable and Uncountable Nouns

You know that a noun names a person, place, thing, or idea. It's usually easy to tell whether nouns referring to people, places, and things are singular or plural because they are usually **countable**. You can have one dog, three cousins, and two radios. You can go to twelve stores in one town.

However, you cannot count some things and ideas. Nouns like *knowledge, pain, love, advice,* and *beauty* are **uncountable**. Uncountable nouns are singular. If you put a pronoun in the place of an uncountable noun, you use the pronoun *it.*

The subject of the following sentence is an uncountable noun. Replace the uncountable noun with *it.* Underline the verb that correctly completes the sentence.

Knowledge *(increase, increases)* your job skills.

Your knowledge cannot be counted. You can't say, "I have seven knowledges." Since *knowledge* can be replaced by the pronoun *it,* the verb must end in *s.* Here is the correct answer:

It
~~Knowledge~~ *(increase, <u>increases</u>)* your job skills.

EXERCISE 3: SINGULAR AND PLURAL SUBJECTS

Directions: Cross out the subject of each sentence and replace it with *he, she, it,* or *they.* Then underline the correct verb. The first one is done as an example.

1. *It*
   ~~Summer~~ *(are, <u>is</u>)* the best time of the year.

2. Teresa *(love, loves)* New England.

3. Silence *(make, makes)* Daryl nervous.

4. Families *(move, moves)* from city to city.

5. The gardens *(look, looks)* gorgeous.

6. Colorado's ski slopes *(bring, brings)* skiers to the state.

7. Carl *(guide, guides)* tourists through the Everglades.

8. Strength *(give, gives)* a woman confidence.

Check your work on page 207.

TRICKY SUBJECT-VERB AGREEMENT

Sometimes it's a little hard to tell exactly how to make a subject and a verb agree. This is especially true when the subject of a sentence has two parts or when phrases come between the subject and the verb. In this part of the chapter, you'll learn to handle these subject-verb agreement problems.

When a sentence has a **compound subject**, the subject is in two parts, which are always connected by *and, or,* or *nor.* The parts are always nouns or pronouns. This sentence has a compound subject:

Ed and Joe like to eat breakfast at the local diner.

In that sentence, *Ed* and *Joe* are the two parts of the compound subject. The two parts are joined by *and.*

In the next example, the two parts of the compound subject are joined by *or.* See if you can identify and underline the two parts of the compound subject.

Either Alice or I have to plan the surprise party for our boss.

The two parts of the compound subject in that sentence are *Alice* and *I.* (*Either* is not part of the subject.)

Underline the parts of the compound subjects in the sentences below.

Karen and Carol love Chinese food.

Mrs. Jones and her daughter love Italian food.

The adults or the teenagers bring the snacks.

Neither she nor her brother is likely to win the contest.

You should have underlined *Karen* and *Carol*, *Mrs. Jones* and *her daughter*, *The adults* and *the teenagers*, and *she* and *her brother*. (The words *either* and *neither* often appear with compound subjects, but they are never part of the subject.)

Now that you can identify compound subjects, you can learn how to make verbs agree with compound subjects.

Compound Subjects Joined by *And*

Very often, the parts of a compound subject are joined by the word *and*.

> Compound subjects joined by *and* are always plural. They need a verb that agrees with a plural subject.

Remember, a plural subject needs a verb that does *not* end in _____.

Here are some examples. Underline the parts of the compound subject and circle the verb in each sentence. The first one is done for you.

<u>Music</u> and <u>art</u> (excite) many people.

Football and baseball thrill millions of sports fans.

Susan and I love movies.

You should have underlined *Football* and *baseball* in the second sentence and *Susan* and *I* in the third sentence. You should have circled *thrill* in the second sentence and *love* in the third sentence. Notice that none of the verbs in the three sentences end in *s*.

Compound Subjects Joined by *Or* or *Nor*

Deciding which verb to use when the parts of a compound subject are joined by *or* or *nor* takes a little more thought.

> When a compound subject is joined by *or* or *nor*, the verb has to agree with the subject that is closest to the verb.

Underline the two parts of the compound subject in the following sentence. Which part is closest to the verb?

Either Betsy or you **come** home at 3:00 every day.

The two parts of the subject are *Betsy* and *you*. The part of the subject closest to the verb is *you*. According to the subject-verb agreement rule, the pronoun *you* needs a verb that does not end in *s*.

Now look at the sentence again, this time with the parts of the subject switched:

Either you or Betsy **comes** home at 3:00 every day.

Since the part of the subject closest to the verb now is *Betsy*, the form of the verb must agree with a singular subject. According to the subject-verb agreement rule, the singular noun *Betsy* needs a verb ending in *s*.

When the parts of the subject are joined by *nor*, the verb is chosen the same way. The verb agrees with the part of the subject closest to it. Underline the two parts of the compound subject in the following sentence. Then circle the verb that agrees with the closest part of the subject.

Neither Max nor his brothers *(plan, plans)* to visit Mother.

The two parts of the compound subject are *Max* and *his brothers*. The correct verb is *plan*, which agrees with the closest part of the subject, *his brothers*. Remember, a plural subject needs a verb that does not end in *s*.

Now look at the sentence again with the parts of the subject reversed. Circle the verb that agrees with the closest part of the subject in the new sentence.

Neither his brothers nor Max *(plan, plans)* to visit Mother.

The correct verb for that sentence is *plans*, which agrees with the singular subject *Max*. Remember, a singular subject needs a verb that ends in *s*.

Complete the Following

Compound subjects joined by the word *and* are always _____.

A plural subject needs a verb that does not end in _____.

When compound subjects are joined by *or* or *nor*, the verb has to agree

with the subject that is _____ to the verb.

EXERCISE 4: SUBJECT-VERB AGREEMENT WITH COMPOUND SUBJECTS

Directions: Underline the parts of the compound subject in each sentence. Then circle the correct form of the verb. The first one is done as an example.

1. The local police and the state police *((increase,* increases)* their patrols on holiday weekends.

2. Relatives or a friend *(is, are)* likely to visit me on Sunday.

3. Henry and his sisters *(come, comes)* every year.

4. You and your parents *(need, needs)* to spend more time together.

5. Neither Nan nor I *(go, goes)* to Canada for Christmas.

6. A local club or businesses *(give, gives)* awards for community service.

7. Neither coffee nor sweets *(have, has)* any nutritional value.

8. Newspapers and radio *(help, helps)* people stay informed.

Check your work on page 207.

PUTTING YOUR SKILLS TO WORK

Directions: Take out your writing folder or notebook again. You are now going to write ten sentences using compound subjects. You may write about anything or anyone you wish. Write carefully and correctly, using the skills you have learned in this book. Pay close attention to subject-verb agreement.

In at least two of your sentences, join the parts of the compound subject with the word *and*. In at least two other sentences, use *or* to connect the parts of the subject. In at least two other sentences, use *nor*. Remember, you need to write a total of ten sentences.

Start writing your sentences. Write neatly and remember to date your writing.

☑ Writing Checklist

❑ Do you have at least two sentences using and, two sentences using or, and two sentences using nor?
❑ Do the verbs agree with the subjects?

Complete the Following

In the present tense, the verb must end in _____ if the subject is *he,*

she, it, or a _____ noun. If the subject is _____, _____, _____,

_____, or a plural noun, the verb does not end in _____.

DESCRIBING PHRASES

In many sentences, describing phrases come between the subject and the verb. Sometimes a describing phrase can make it hard to tell what the subject is. To make sure the subject and verb agree, you must be able to find the subject and ignore the describing phrase. Here's an example of a sentence with a describing phrase between the subject and the verb.

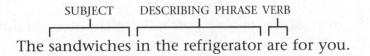

SUBJECT   DESCRIBING PHRASE VERB

The sandwiches in the refrigerator are for you.

In that sentence, the subject, *sandwiches,* is plural. The verb *are* is correct for a plural subject. Notice that the describing phrase, *in the refrigerator,* does not affect subject-verb agreement.

Here is another example. Circle the subject and the verb in the following sentence. Cross out the describing phrase between the subject and the verb.

The man on roller blades falls often.

If you are having any trouble finding the subject, first find the verb. The verb is *falls*. Now ask yourself, "Who or what falls often?" The answer is the subject, *man*. Now you know that the subject and the verb agree, since the singular subject *man* needs a verb ending in *s*. You should have crossed out the describing phrase *on roller blades*, which does not affect subject-verb agreement.

Now try making the subject and verb agree in a sentence with a describing phrase. Circle the subject of the following sentence and cross out the describing phrase. Then underline the verb that agrees with the subject.

The hinges on the door *(are, is)* rusty.

The subject is *hinges*. The describing phrase is *on the door*. The verb must agree with the plural subject *hinges*, so the correct form is *are*.

Your common sense can help you with a sentence like that one. It makes sense that the hinges would be rusty, so *hinges* has to be the subject of the sentence.

Now try one more example. Circle the subject of the following sentence and cross out the describing phrase. Then underline the verb that agrees with the subject.

A car with bucket seats *(hold, holds)* fewer passengers.

The correct verb is *holds*. The subject is *car*, a singular noun. The describing phrase is *with bucket seats*.

EXERCISE 5: SUBJECT-VERB AGREEMENT WITH DESCRIBING PHRASES

Directions: Circle the subject of each sentence. Cross out the describing phrase. Then choose the correct verb to agree with the subject. Remember to follow the subject-verb agreement rule. The first one is done as an example.

1. The (tree) ~~with the red and gold leaves~~ *(change, changes)* color in early October.

2. The children under the tree *(pick, picks)* up the colorful leaves.

3. The teacher in the green slacks *(watch, watches)* the children carefully.

4. The father of one of the girls *(arrive, arrives)* early today.

5. Truckers with good sense *(take, takes)* safety precautions.

6. A truck with bad brakes *(have, has)* to be repaired immediately.

7. A driver on a long trip *(go, goes)* to a truck stop to rest.

8. Truck stops on the freeway *(is, are)* busy all night long.

Check your work on page 207.

PUTTING YOUR SKILLS TO WORK

Directions: Use what you have learned in this chapter as you do the following assignment in your writing folder or notebook. Don't forget to date your writing.

Write a paragraph about a familiar group or organization. It might be your softball team or a local club. Perhaps you are a great fan of the Dallas Cowboys, the Cincinnati Bengals, or a local school's hockey or track team. If you belong to a church or synagogue, a girls' or boys' club, or a neighborhood organization, you could write about that. Or, if you are enrolled in a class, you could write about your class.

Before you write your paragraph, try brainstorming about the group you are going to describe. (You can review brainstorming on pages 96–97). Use ideas from your brainstorm in your paragraph.

☑ *Writing Checklist*

❑ Do all your subjects and verbs agree? Have you used correct verb forms?

❑ Have you referred to singular nouns with singular pronouns and plural nouns with plural pronouns?

EXERCISE 6: SUBJECT-VERB AGREEMENT REVIEW

Directions: In this exercise, you will practice all the subject-verb agreement skills you have learned in this chapter. Underline the correct verb to complete each sentence.

1. Nutritious meals and rest *(help, helps)* sick people recover.

2. They *(am, is, are)* registered to vote.

3. Clerks in that store *(say, says)* the work is hard.

4. Sally *(believe, believes)* what she hears on TV.

5. A grandmother and grandfather *(give, gives)* tender loving care to their grandchildren.

6. Those blankets *(go, goes)* on Maggie's bed.

7. You *(do, does)* not have a chance of getting away with that.

8. Neither the vegetables nor the meat *(look, looks)* good to me.

9. Women in the job training program *(earn, earns)* wages for going to class.

10. Either a colorful poster or flowers *(cheer, cheers)* up a bare office.

Check your work on pages 207–208.

 PUNCTUATING PERFECTLY

COMMAS

Commas have many uses. They can be used to interrupt the sentence with additional information, to connect or make transitions between ideas, or to address a person directly.

Commas for Additional Information

When additional information is given about the subject of a sentence, commas are used to set off the information. Notice how a comma comes before and after the additional information in the following example.

Mrs. Stiffler, **my sixth-grade teacher**, really loved teaching.

In that sentence, the phrase *my sixth-grade teacher* is set off by commas. The phrase interrupts the sentence to give more information about Mrs. Stiffler.

Here is another example. In the following sentence, the phrase that gives additional information comes at the end of the sentence, so only one comma is needed.

One of my best friends is Harry, **the barber on Ninth Street**.

In that sentence, the phrase *the barber on Ninth Street* gives more information about Harry.

In the following sentence, a noun is underlined. Add two commas to the sentence to set off the phrase that gives additional information about the underlined noun.

<u>Ms. Tortelli</u> the pizza shop owner loves French food.

You should have put a comma after *Ms. Tortelli* and after *owner*. The phrase that gives additional information about Ms. Tortelli is *the pizza shop owner.*

Now try another example. This time the noun is not underlined. Add one comma to the following sentence to set off the phrase that gives the additional information.

The best person for that job is Ben an experienced carpenter.

Did you put a comma after *Ben*? The phrase that gives the additional information is *an experienced carpenter*. A phrase that gives additional information always comes directly after the noun it describes.

When you punctuate a phrase that gives additional information, always be careful to put a comma both before *and* after the phrase, unless it comes at the end of the sentence. Here is a common error to avoid:

INCORRECT: Ben, an experienced carpenter can do the job.
CORRECT: Ben, an experienced carpenter, can do the job.

EXERCISE 7: COMMAS WITH PHRASES THAT GIVE ADDITIONAL INFORMATION

Directions: Find the phrase that gives additional information in each of these sentences. Use commas to set off each phrase from the rest of the sentence. The first one is done as an example.

1. The Wizard of Oz, a favorite childhood character, granted wishes.

2. Checkers a game for two is challenging for children and adults.

3. I like to have a hamburger or two at Moody's a local drive-in.

4. Horror films a frightening form of entertainment attract big audiences.

5. The undercover policeman on the case is Detective Blackwell a member of the vice squad.

6. Linda Chavez the Republican candidate lost the election.

Check your work on page 208.

Commas for Connecting Ideas or Making Transitions

Commas are also used to set off short interrupting phrases that connect or make transitions between ideas in a sentence. The following sentences contain examples of these short phrases. Notice that, if you take out the words between the commas, the sentence still tells a complete thought.

I could, **for example**, move to San Francisco.
I might, **on the other hand**, move to Phoenix.

In those sentences, the interrupting phrases come in the middle of the sentence. Two commas are needed—one before and one after the interrupting phrase. However, these phrases could also come at the beginning or the end of the sentence.

I could move to San Francisco, **for example**.
On the other hand, I might move to Phoenix.

Notice that, when the interrupting phrases are moved to the beginning or end of the sentence, only one comma is needed.

Here is a list of common interrupting phrases that connect or make transitions between ideas.

of course	for example
in my opinion	in fact
by the way	on one hand
	on the other hand

Put commas where they are needed in the following sentences to set off interrupting phrases.

The rumor about Diana is in my opinion totally untrue.
In fact she was at her sister's house all last week.

In the first sentence, you should have put a comma before *in* and after *opinion*. In the second sentence, a comma is needed after *fact*.

EXERCISE 8: PHRASES THAT CONNECT OR MAKE TRANSITIONS BETWEEN IDEAS

Directions: Put commas where they are needed in the following sentences to set off the interrupting phrases. The first one is done as an example.

1. My best friend, of course, would never go out with my boyfriend.

2. On one hand Bruce wants very much to have children.

3. On the other hand he is worried about all the responsibility.

4. I just learned in fact that I'm eating all the wrong foods.

5. Marlene gave up smoking by the way.

6. Andy in my opinion is not mature enough to live on his own.

Check your work on page 208.

Commas for Direct Address

Names used in *direct address* are set off by commas. When you use a person's name to speak directly to him or her, the name is set off by commas. For example, if you were asking Charles to help you, you could write this sentence:

Charles, would you please help with this project?

A comma sets off the name *Charles* in that sentence. Only one comma is needed because the name comes first in the sentence.

In the following example, the name used in direct address comes in the middle of the sentence. Two commas are needed to set off *Mr. Littlefield*. Put the commas where they belong.

I hope Mr. Littlefield that you will accept this offer.

You should have put a comma both before and after *Mr. Littlefield*.

The name could also come at the end of the sentence, as in this example. Place a comma where it belongs.

You had better think twice about that Fred.

You should have put a comma before *Fred*.

EXERCISE 9: COMMAS IN DIRECT ADDRESS

Directions: Insert commas in these sentences. The first one is done for you.

1. Terry, will you please come for a visit this summer?

2. If I could afford the trip Mary I would surely come.

3. Mr. Gregson you are a very lucky man.

4. Do you realize how talented you are Paula?

5. In two weeks Mrs. Grant your lease will expire.

Check your work on page 208.

EXERCISE 10: REVIEW OF COMMAS

Directions: Add the necessary comma or commas to these sentences. You will need to recognize phrases that give additional information, phrases that connect ideas or make transitions, and names used in direct address. The first one is done as an example.

1. Tim, my first cousin, is coming to live with us.

2. He arrives tomorrow in fact.

3. Mrs. Brown the lady across the street said she might be able to get him a job.

4. We hope Ms. Coleman that you are prepared for the worst.

5. Will you work overtime Beth?

6. Life in a big city is of course both exciting and scary.

7. Felix a friend from my hometown convinced me to go back to school.

Check your work on page 208.

PUTTING YOUR SKILLS TO WORK

Directions: Take out your writing folder or notebook again. This time you will be writing a series of sentences.

1. Write two sentences with phrases that give additional information. Make certain you use commas correctly. Here is an example:

   Danielle, an eighth-grader, is taking piano lessons.

2. Write two sentences with phrases that connect or make transitions between ideas. Use commas carefully. You can choose from the list of phrases on page 112. Here is an example:

   Television, in my opinion, is not worth watching.

3. Write two sentences showing direct address. Be careful about comma placement. Here is an example:

   Woody, you are acting like a fool!

☑ *Writing Checklist*

❏ Do you have two sentences showing the use of commas with phrases that give additional information?

❏ Do you have two sentences showing phrases that connect ideas? Are the phrases set off by commas?

❏ Do you have two sentences showing the use of commas with direct address?

❏ Do the subjects of your sentences agree with the verbs?

EXERCISE 11: CHAPTER REVIEW

Part 1

To complete this part of the review, you will need to use the information you studied in this chapter.

Directions: Complete the following.

1. What is subject-verb agreement? _____

_____

2. To agree with the subject pronouns *he, she,* and *it*, a verb in the

present tense must _____

3. To agree with a plural subject, a verb in the present tense must not ___

_____.

4. What is a compound subject? _____

_____

Directions: Find the mistake in each of the following sentences and correct it. If a word needs to be changed, cross out the wrong word and write the correct word above it. If there is a mistake in punctuation, add the correct punctuation or cross out the incorrect punctuation. The first one is done as an example.

5. Lucas and Dena ~~wants~~ *want* to buy a house.

6. They is looking on the east side of town.

7. A porch or patio give a house an outdoor feeling.

8. Lucas, an excellent cook examines the kitchens carefully.

9. Sunlight are important to Dena.

10. The house with the hardwood floors were too expensive.

11. Neither Lucas nor Dena like the less expensive houses.

12. They are in fact, afraid that they will never find a good house for what they can pay.

Part 2

In this part of the review, you will use all of the information you have studied throughout this book.

Directions: Complete the following.

1. What is the difference between a common noun and a proper noun?

   _____

   _____

2. What is the difference between a sentence and a fragment?

   _____

   _____

3. What do you add to a singular noun to make it possessive? _____

4. What helping verb is used to form the future tense? _____

Directions: Find the mistake in each sentence. On the blank line, rewrite the sentence correctly.

5. Bobs car looks brand-new.

   _____

6. He is very careful to maintain it properly

   _____

7. the required oil change is done every 3,000 miles.

   _____

8. Him rotates the tires every 7,500 miles.

   _____

9. Last month, he change the gas filter, the oil, and the spark plugs.

   _____

10. The best thing to do for a car

    _____

11. A well-kept car will lasted for years.

    _____

12. It's paint can be preserved with regular waxing.

    _____

Check your work on pages 208–209.

YOUR TURN TO WRITE
AN EVENT IN YOUR LIFE

Take out your writing folder or notebook again. This time you will write three paragraphs about an event in your life. You can choose an event as common as a typical workday or as special as a wedding day.

WRITING ASSIGNMENT

Directions: Pick an event that can be divided three ways. In your first paragraph, tell what happened before the event. In your second paragraph, tell what happened during the event. In the third paragraph, tell what happened after the event.

Be sure to indent each of your paragraphs. *Indenting* means starting the first word of a paragraph a few extra spaces to the right.

If you choose to write about a typical school day, your first paragraph will tell what happens before you get to school.

Your second paragraph should tell about the things that happen while you are at school. How many hours are you there? What is your lunchtime like? How does your day end?

Your final paragraph could tell about the things that you do on your way home. It could also tell what you do after you get home.

Here is a list of other possible events for your paragraphs. Remember, your job is to tell what happened before, during, and after. Write neatly and correctly. Be especially careful with verbs and commas.

1. A holiday celebration
2. Interviewing for a job
3. The first date with _____
4. The first day of school
5. Moving to a new home
6. Your choice

☑ Writing Checklist

❏ Are each of your three paragraphs indented?

❏ Do you have commas in the right places?

❏ Do your subjects and verbs agree?

C H A P T E R   6

JOURNAL WRITING
STATING YOUR OPINION

Forming an opinion is an art that you can develop by sorting out your thoughts and ideas about a subject. Your opinion is what you think about something. You are allowed to think whatever you want. Your opinion on any subject is based on facts, on ideas, and on information you have received from a number of sources. You also form opinions through personal experiences.

Since your journal is private, it is a good place to explore your opinions freely. You can practice sorting out thoughts and using examples and ideas to support your opinions. In this journal entry, you will give your opinion about an issue.

For example, you might want to give your opinion about whether or not the schools in your neighborhood or city need more teachers. Your information sources might include your school experiences. You may have read articles or seen television news stories about your local schools. Finally, perhaps you may have friends who go to a different school. You may be comparing their school with your school. For this journal entry, you could combine all these impressions to support an opinion statement.

JOURNAL ENTRY

Directions: For this journal entry, you can choose one of the following opinion statements to write about. Choose one you agree with and have something to say about. You can also make up your own opinion statement. Write the opinion statement you are going to use at the top of a page in your journal.

Our school system needs more teachers.
Teachers should be paid higher salaries.
Teenagers should not be allowed to drop out of high school.
Sex education should not be taught in the public schools.

Next, have a brainstorming session. Write down all the ways you can think of to support your opinion statement. Try to think of lots of arguments and specific details and examples. Then read over your work and mark the ideas you want to include in your writing.

Finally, on the next page, write your opinion sentence again. Follow it with sentences that support your opinion.

LANGUAGE SKILLS
ADJECTIVES AND ADVERBS

WHAT IS AN ADJECTIVE?

Adjectives are words that describe nouns. Adjectives tell what kind, which one, or how many. Adjectives make nouns more specific.

For example, if you say, "James bought a motorcycle," you are not being very specific about the type of motorcycle he bought. Here are two different sentences that use adjectives to explain exactly what kind of motorcycle James bought.

James bought a **big**, **black**, **shiny** motorcycle.
James bought a **small**, **red**, **inexpensive**, **used** motorcycle.

In both sentences, you learn that James bought a motorcycle, but there is a big difference between the motorcycle described in the first sentence and the one described in the second sentence. The adjectives make each sentence more specific.

Here are three lists of adjectives that are used very often. To see more examples of adjectives, you also can turn back to page 18 in the first chapter.

What Kind	Which One	How Many
tiny, silly, right, sleepy, loud, fast, tight, long	this, that, these, those	none, some, a dozen, much, fourteen (any number)

Using adjectives from the lists above, fill in the blanks in the following sentences.

After driving ___*that*___ truck for _____ hours, Tim
          (which one)   *(how many)*

was _____.
     (what kind)

The _____ dentist has told _____ jokes at least
     (what kind)   *(which ones)*

_____ times.
  (how many)

Your sentences should be similar to these:

After driving **that** truck for **fourteen** hours, Tim was **sleepy**.
The **silly** dentist has told **those** jokes at least **a dozen** times.

Adjectives make sentences more specific and more interesting. For example, you can say, "I have a dog," or you can say, "I have a tiny, friendly, curly-haired dog with a ferocious bark." The second sentence is more specific and gives the listener a much better picture of the dog.

The more specific an adjective is, the better it describes what you are talking about. Below are five adjectives. Next to each one, list at least three other adjectives that could describe someone or something more specifically. You can look up the words in a dictionary to get ideas.

Small: _*tiny, undersized, trivial*_____

Nice: _____

Pretty: _____

Good: _____

Big: _____

EXERCISE 1: CHOOSING ADJECTIVES

Directions: Choose adjectives from the list below to fill in the blanks. Some of the adjectives can be used in more than one of the sentences. The first one is done as an example.

hectic, busy, many, frustrated, small, colorful, expensive, inexpensive, gigantic, numerous

1. ___*Hectic*___ shopping takes place during holidays.

2. The _____ stores are overcrowded.

3. In the evening, _____ customers pack the stores.

4. _____ clerks have too much work to do.

5. During a sale, bargain hunters fight over _____ purchases.

6. _____ lights decorate the stores.

7. Children sometimes ask for _____ presents.

8. Often parents can afford only _____ presents.

9. Trying to satisfy a child's requests can cause _____ bills.

10. _____ parents have learned it's OK to say no to a child's unreasonable request.

Check your work on page 209.

EXERCISE 2: USING ADJECTIVES

Directions: Fill in each blank in the following sentences with an adjective. The adjective should describe the underlined noun next to the blank. Part of the first one is done as an example.

1. The ___*middle-aged*___ <u>men</u> play_____ <u>games</u> of poker
      (what kind)   (how many)
   once a month.

2. They use _____ <u>cards</u> and play on a _____ <u>table</u>.
            (what kind)   (what kind)

3. The game is played on the _____ Friday of each month.
　　　　　　　　　　　　　　　　(which one)

4. The bets are _____ .
　　　　　　　　　　(what kind)

5. During the _____ game, _____ pounds
　　　　　　　　　(what kind)　　　　　　　　　(how many)
of potato chips are eaten.

Check your work on page 209.

PUTTING YOUR SKILLS TO WORK

Directions: Take out your notebook again. You are going to practice using adjectives in this assignment. First, do a quick brainstorming exercise. At the top of a sheet of paper, write your name or the name of a close friend or relative. Then write the first ten adjectives you can think of to describe the person you named. Finally, use at least five of those adjectives and write a paragraph about the person.

Here is a sample paragraph from a student's list that contained the adjectives *thoughtful, loving, funny, disorganized,* and *oldest.*

> Martha is a very **thoughtful** person who never forgets to send birthday cards. She is a **loving** person and a **funny** lady. However, she is also very **disorganized.** She is the **oldest** employee in her company, yet the boss refuses to let her retire.

That student used five adjectives. You may use as many as you like, but use at least five. Be sure to date your entry. Decide which adjective you want to use first and start writing.

☑ *Writing Checklist*

❏ Have you included five adjectives from your list?

❏ Do your sentences start with capital letters?

❏ Does each sentence have a punctuation mark at the end?

Complete the Following

Adjectives are words that _____ _____. Adjectives

tell _____, _____, or _____. Adjectives make

nouns _____ _____.

(You may go back to page 120 for help with the definition.)

WHERE DO ADJECTIVES BELONG?

An adjective often comes right before the noun it describes, as in this example:

The **happy** child ran through the house.

However, an adjective often can be found in another part of a sentence. You can tell it is an adjective because it describes the noun. It still tells you what kind, which one, or how many. Here are two examples:

Tina is happy.

Write the word that describes Tina on this blank. _____
Even though the word *happy* does not come before *Tina*, it is an adjective because it describes what kind of person she is.

Francis is next.

Write the word that describes Francis on this blank. _____
The word *next* follows the verb, but it describes Francis by telling which place he is in. Therefore, *next* is an adjective.

EXERCISE 3: IDENTIFYING ADJECTIVES

Directions: The adjectives in the following sentences may come right before the nouns they describe, but they may not. Circle the adjective in each sentence. The noun that the adjective describes is underlined. The first one is done as an example.

1. Television can be (educational.)

2. The news is informative.

3. Many people watch the news.

4. Sometimes tired viewers go to sleep.

5. Silly soap operas air daily.

6. Sometimes their plots are absurd.

7. The characters do stupid things.

8. These shows go on for years.

9. Shows about police and detectives are popular.

10. However, they can be violent.

Check your work on page 209.

WHAT IS AN ADVERB?

Adverbs are words that describe verbs. Adverbs can tell how, when, or where.

Here are three lists of adverbs.

How	When	Where
rapidly	today	outside
angrily	later	inside
happily	daily	there
fast	once	here
slowly	again	

Just as adjectives give more information about nouns, adverbs tell you more about verbs. Look at this sentence, which does not contain any adverbs.

Lynn will talk.

That sentence doesn't tell how, when, or where Lynn will talk. By adding an adverb after the verb *talk* you can give more specific information about the verb. The sentence has been rewritten below with two different adverbs. Continue rewriting the sentence until you have two sentences with adverbs that tell *how*, two sentences with adverbs that tell *when*, and two sentences with adverbs that tell *where*. You may use adverbs from the lists above.

Lynn will talk ___*slowly*___. (how)

Lynn will talk ___*later*___. (when)

Lynn will talk _____. (where)

Lynn will talk _____. (how)

Lynn will talk _____. (when)

Lynn will talk _____. (where)

Now that you have used six adverbs from the list, see if you can write one of each type using adverbs of your own.

Leon will walk _____. (how)

Leon will walk _____. (when)

Leon will walk _____. (where)

EXERCISE 4: CHOOSING ADVERBS

Directions: Choose an adverb from the list below to describe each verb. Write the adverb in the blank. You will discover that it is possible to use some of the adverbs in more than one place. The first one is done as an example.

hysterically, before, outside, patiently, strangely, rapidly, down, threateningly, nervously, abruptly

1. Andrew laughed _____.

2. He smiled _____ the show started.

3. He grinned _____ the theatre.

4. His mother stood _____ waiting for him to stop laughing.

5. People looked _____ at him.

6. Tears flowed _____ from his eyes.

7. He laughed so much, he fell _____.

8. "Get up, Andrew," his mother said _____.

9. "I can't," he giggled _____.

10. "No one would understand," he stated _____ and then continued laughing.

Check your work on page 209.

EXERCISE 5: WRITING SENTENCES WITH ADVERBS

Directions: In this exercise you will write three groups of sentences. In each group of sentences, you will use an adverb that tells *how*, an adverb that tells *when*, and an adverb that tells *where*. One from each group is done as an example.

1. In this group, use adverbs with the verb *write*.

    a. *(how)* _____

    b. *(when)* _We write daily._____

    c. *(where)* _____

2. In this group, use adverbs with the verb *dance.*

    a. *(how)* _Melinda and Todd dance beautifully._____

    b. *(when)* _____

    c. *where)* _____

3. Finally, in this group, use adverbs with the verb *read.*

    a. *(how)* _____

    b. *(when)* _____

    c. *(where)* _Sam will read here._____

Check your work on pages 209–210.

Complete the Following

Adverbs are words that _____ _____. Adverbs can tell

_____, _____, or _____.

Adjectives and adverbs are alike because they both describe other words.

Adjectives describe _____, and adverbs describe _____.

WHERE DO ADVERBS APPEAR?

    So far, you have seen that an adverb can come right after the verb it describes. But often an adverb will be found in another part of the sentence. You can tell it is an adverb because it still describes the verb. It tells you how, where, or when. Here are three examples.

        Angrily, she turned her back to the group.

On this line, write the word that tells *how* she turned. _____
Even though the adverb is the first word in the sentence, *angrily* still describes the verb—it tells how.

        Eric bought a car today.

Write the word that tells *when* he bought the car. _____
Although *today* does not come right after the verb *bought*, it is an adverb describing the verb—it tells when.

        Last night, the softball team won first place here.

Write the word that tells *where* the softball team won. _____
The adverb *here* is separated from the verb, but it still describes the verb—it tells where the players were when they won.

EXERCISE 6: IDENTIFYING ADVERBS

Directions: Circle the adverb in each of the following sentences. There is one adverb in each sentence. The verb that the adverb describes is underlined. The first one is done as an example.

1. Commuters <u>drive</u> (far) to work.

2. Some <u>leave</u> early to miss traffic jams.

3. Many dangerously <u>ignore</u> the speed limit.

4. They <u>watch</u> carefully for speed traps.

5. Mysteriously, police <u>appear</u> to give tickets.

6. After getting a ticket, the commuter <u>drives</u> angrily to work.

7. Calmly, the trooper <u>will wait</u> for the next speeder.

8. A commuter can <u>look</u> everywhere and still not see the police.

9. The police car <u>is</u> there.

10. A safe commuter always <u>travels</u> as if a traffic patrolman were his passenger.

Check your work on page 210.

Complete the Following

Adverbs are words that _____ _____. Adverbs can tell _____,

_____, or _____.

ADJECTIVE OR ADVERB?

Adjectives and adverbs are both words that describe. In many cases, they are almost alike. Often a word that is an adjective can be changed to an adverb by adding two letters. These letters are *ly*. Here are two examples:

Adjective	Adverb
sad	sadly
beautiful	beautifully

However, if an adjective ends in *y*, you must change the *y* to *i* and then add the *ly*. Here are two examples:

Adjective	Adverb
angry	angrily
happy	happily

Here are adjectives and adverbs that are very much alike. Circle the adverbs in which *y* is changed to *i*.

Adjective	Adverb
brave	bravely
calm	calmly
hungry	hungrily
general	generally
busy	busily
mysterious	mysteriously
sad	sadly
thoughtful	thoughtfully
usual	usually

The way a word is used in a sentence tells you whether to use the adjective or the adverb form. If you want to describe a noun, use an adjective. If you want to describe a verb, use an adverb.

Here are some examples showing when to use the adjective and adverb forms.

The **sad** man walked down the street.
The man walked **sadly** down the street.

What word is described in the first sentence? _____

What word is described in the second sentence? _____

The first sentence tells what kind of man walked. Since *sad* describes a noun *(man)*, it is an adjective. The second sentence tells how the man walked. Since *sadly* describes a verb *(walked)*, it is an adverb.

Shelley followed her **usual** route.
Shelley **usually** followed this route.

What word is described in the first sentence? _____

What word is described in the second sentence? _____

In the first sentence, *usual* describes *route*. It tells what kind of route, so it is an adjective. In the second sentence, *usually* describes *followed*. It tells when Shelley followed the route, so it is an adverb.

Complete the Following

Many times, an adjective can be changed to an adverb by adding the

letters _____ to the end of the word. On the following line, write three

adjectives that can be changed to adverbs by adding *ly*. _____

_____

When an adjective ends in *y*, to change it to an adverb, you must

change the _____ to an _____ and add _____ to the end of the word.

EXERCISE 7: CHOOSING ADJECTIVES OR ADVERBS

Directions: Underline the correct form for each sentence. One of the choices is an adjective, and the other is an adverb. If you are describing a noun, choose the adjective. If you are describing a verb, choose the adverb. The first one is done as an example.

1. Football season is *(fantastic, fantastically)* for the avid sports fan.

2. A fan prepares *(careful, carefully)* for each game.

3. He waits *(calm, calmly)* for the whistle that starts the game.

4. Around him, the *(excited, excitedly)* crowd cheers for their team.

5. He applauds *(loud, loudly)* when his team makes a touchdown.

6. The people around him turn *(angry, angrily)* and stare at him.

7. *(Sudden, Suddenly)* he realizes he is in enemy territory.

8. His *(cheerful, cheerfully)* smile wins over those close to him.

9. The game becomes *(interesting, interestingly)* as the score ties.

10. Ten seconds before the end of the game, a quarterback throws a *(magnificent, magnificently)* pass for a touchdown catch, and the fan goes home grinning.

Check your work on page 210.

| PUNCTUATING PERFECTLY |

COMMAS IN A SERIES

Sometimes in your writing you may want to use several adjectives or adverbs to describe one noun or verb. How can you punctuate the series of adjectives or adverbs? Use commas to separate three or more items in a series. Here are some examples:

The **large, green, spotted, worm-eaten** apple fell from the tree.

Adjectives describing the apple are separated by commas in that sentence.

The chorus began **slowly, carefully, quietly,** and **harmoniously**.

That sentence contains four adverbs that tell how the chorus began. The adverbs are separated by commas.

Where would you place commas in the following sentence, which contains three adverbs? Write them in where they are missing.

Nina Totenberg speaks calmly clearly and firmly.

You were right if you put commas after *calmly* and *clearly*. Make sure you did not put a comma after *speaks*.

Now try another example. This time you'll punctuate a sentence containing four adjectives. Put commas where they are missing in the following sentence.

The long modern sleek curved building won an award for its design.

You should have put commas after *long, modern,* and *sleek*. Check to be sure you did not use any extra commas.

In addition to adjectives and adverbs, other kinds of words can be used in series. In the following example, three nouns make up a series. Underline the items in the series. Notice how commas separate the items.

Please bring coffee, tea, and cream to the meeting.

In that sentence, the items *coffee, tea,* and *cream* are separated by commas. Notice that no comma is placed before the first item *(coffee)* or after the last item *(cream)*.

Remember this rule for using commas in a series.

> Commas are used after every item except the last one in a series of three or more items.

It is also very important to remember not to use a comma between only two items. Here are two examples:

Jan and Mark are working today.

Since Jan and Mark are only two people, no comma appears between them.

Cincinnati or Austin will host the next cowhands convention.

Since only two cities are listed, no comma is used.

Read the three sentences that follow. Add commas where necessary. Be sure not to add any extra commas.

George swims runs and lifts weights to stay in shape.

The Tigers and the Redskins will play a game on Monday.

Joan searched carefully endlessly and fruitlessly for her lost contact lens.

The first sentence contains a series of three verbs—*swims, runs,* and *lifts.* You should have put commas after *swims* and *runs.* The second sentence needs no commas since only two teams are named. In the third sentence, two commas are needed, one after *carefully* and one after *endlessly.*

Complete the Following

What is the rule for using commas in a series?

_____

_____

EXERCISE 8: USING COMMAS IN A SERIES

Directions: Add commas to the following sentences wherever they are needed. Some sentences may not need any commas.

1. The women's club is planning a dinner and a play to celebrate its anniversary.

2. Also included in the program will be speakers awards and music.

3. Sue Almeda Fran Warner Lillian Rutledge and Vanessa Grogan are in charge of inviting guests.

4. Interested enthusiastic dedicated volunteers will be invited.

5. Their husbands or escorts will be invited too.

6. The club must plan for feeding and entertaining 250 adults.

7. On the menu will be stuffed chicken breasts baked potatoes peas salad rolls ice cream and coffee.

8. The play will require the cooperation of talented interested well-rehearsed participants.

9. It will include poetry dialogue songs and music.

10. The volunteers to be honored work daily weekly or monthly at a variety of tasks.

Check your work on page 210.

EXERCISE 9: WRITING SENTENCES WITH SERIES
Directions: Write sentences containing series (or lists) in response to the following. Make certain that you have at least three items separated by commas in each sentence.

1. Write a sentence listing what you will have for supper one day this week.

    _____

2. Write a sentence using adjectives describing an interesting person you

    know. _____

3. Write a sentence describing how a child reacted to circus clowns. _____

    _____

Check your work on page 210.

PUNCTUATING LETTERS

In your daily life, you may find you want to write two kinds of letters. One is a personal letter. The other is a business letter. A personal letter is written to stay in touch with someone, to invite someone to an event, or to thank someone for a gift or a kindness. A business letter is written to take care of a business matter. You might need to write one to apply for a job, order a gift, or complain about a product or service.

Writing a Personal Letter

When you write a personal letter, commas are used in a number of places. You need to know how to use commas correctly in the date, the greeting, and the closing of the letter.

Study this sample personal letter. The commas have been circled.

July 14, 1996   DATE

Dear Georgette,   GREETING

      It has been a long time since I wrote to you. Everyone in the neighborhood misses you. We wish you had not moved away. We would like you to visit us this summer. Can you stay with me from August 7   BODY through August 15? I will look forward to your answer. If you can be here, we can go to the local block party.

Love,   CLOSING

Samantha   SIGNATURE

Commas are used in three places in the sample personal letter:

1. A comma is used in the date between the day of the month and the year. (July 14, 1996)
2. A comma is used after the person's name in the greeting. (Dear Georgette,)
3. A comma is used after the closing. (Love,)

The greeting of any letter will always be Dear _____. The closing can vary to fit the person receiving the letter. You can close a personal letter with any appropriate word. Words like *Love, Sincerely, Fondly, Affectionately, Yours truly,* and other expressions you like to use can end a personal letter. The first word of the closing is always capitalized.

Using the sample letter as a guide, rearrange the parts of the following letter so it is set up and punctuated properly. Write in the blanks below.

Affectionately   *Susan*

Thank you for the great record album. It completes my collection of oldies but goodies from the sixties. Maybe you will get to listen to all the songs with me before long.

May 10 1997   Dear Tommy

_____ DATE

_____ GREETING

_____

_____

_____

_____ BODY

_____

_____

_____

_____ CLOSING

_____ SIGNATURE

Writing a Business Letter

A business letter is very similar to a personal letter. However, there are a few more parts to a business letter. It should include your address (called the *return address*), the address you are writing to (called the *inside address*), and a typed or printed name under your signature. Here is a sample business letter. The business letter punctuation marks have been circled.

15 Tulip Place	RETURN
Chicago, IL 60604	ADDRESS
July 14, 1998	DATE

Mr. James West	
Western Fields Inc.	INSIDE
313 East St.	ADDRESS
Chicago, IL 60607	

Dear Mr. West: GREETING

Thank you for interviewing me for the
hostess position in your company's dining
room. After speaking with you, I am sure I
would enjoy working at Western Fields Inc.   BODY
My past food service experience would
make me a valuable asset to the company.
I look forward to hearing from you in the
near future.

Sincerely,   CLOSING

Ramona Jones   SIGNATURE

Ramona Jones   NAME

The business letter format is more detailed than the personal letter format. Here is how punctuation is used:

1. The return address and inside address have a comma between the name of the city and the state (Chicago, IL). In fact, you always put a comma between the name of a city and a state.
2. The greeting has a colon after the man's name (Dear Mr. West:).
3. A comma follows the closing (Sincerely,). More formal words are used as closings in business letters. *Sincerely* and *Yours truly* are very often used.

Read the short business letter that follows. Then, using the letter to Mr. James West as a sample, put in all the missing punctuation.

227 March Ave.
Rockport MA 08642

Dec. 13 1997

Ms. S. J. Reed
Lightner's Logging Co.
234 Pine Rd.
Rockport MA 08642

Dear Ms. Reed
    This is to inform you that the sweater I ordered is too small.
I am returning the sweater to exchange it for a size 44. Please send
the larger sweater right away.

                Sincerely
                Hank Greene
                Hank Greene

Did you place a comma between the city and state in both the return
address and the inside address? Did you place a comma between the day
and the year in the date? Is there a colon after the greeting? Do you have
a comma after the closing? If so, you have correctly punctuated the
letter.

EXERCISE 10: CORRECTING A BUSINESS LETTER

Directions: A short business letter appears below. Five sections have been
blocked off. There is a mistake in each of those sections. On the blank
lines underneath the letter, rewrite the lines correctly. The first one is
done as an example.

                34 Montrose St.
                Foster City CA 94404 ◄———— 1
                Sept. 22 1997 ◄———————— 2

Dr. Morris Green
34 Heart Lane
Foster City CA 94404 ◄———— 3

Dear Dr. Green ◄———————— 4
    Enclosed is a check for $35.00 to cover your monthly visit.
Thank you for taking care of me. I'm glad there are still doctors who
are willing to make house calls.

                Love and kisses, ◄———————— 5
                Maria Rozinski
                Maria Rozinski

1. *Foster City, CA 94404*   4. _____

2. _____   5. _____

3. _____   **Check your work on page 210.**

EXERCISE 11: CHAPTER REVIEW

Part 1

To complete this section of the chapter review, you will use the information you studied in this chapter, including adjectives, adverbs, and rules for using commas.

Directions: Complete the following.

1. Give the definition of an adjective. _____

   _____

2. Give the definition of an adverb. _____

   _____

3. How can adverbs be formed? _____

   _____

4. What is the rule for using commas in a series? _____

   _____

5. List four places in a business letter where a comma must be used.

   _____

   _____

Directions: Find the mistake in each sentence. Circle the mistake and rewrite each sentence correctly in the space provided. The first one is done as an example.

6. Ruth is a (happily) person.

   Ruth is a happy person. _____

7. The race car moved quick around the track.

   _____

8. Nuts bolts wrenches and tools were thrown around the shop.

   _____

9. The men, and the women agreed that life moves too rapidly.

   _____

10. The customers hungryly ate the barbecued chicken.

   _____

11. The business is located in Anchorage Alaska.

_____

12. The old battered rusted truck limped into the station.

_____

13. The trustworthy young bright babysitter raised her fee.

_____

14. The soldier looked brave into the eyes of his captors.

_____

15. The date on the letter was Feb. 14 1995.

_____

Part 2

In this part of the review, you will use all the information you have studied so far in this book.

Directions: Complete the following.

1. What do you usually do to a singular noun to make it show possession?

_____

2. What do you usually do to a plural noun to make it show possession?

_____

3. What are the three types of punctuation that can be found at the end of a sentence?

_____

Directions: In this exercise, a part of each sentence is underlined. After the sentence, you will find three possible ways to write the underlined section. The first choice is always the same as the underlined part of the sentence. Choose the best correction and fill in the box under **a**, **b**, or **c** to indicate your answer. The first one is done as an example.

                             a   **b**   **c**

4. The <u>united states</u> often allows people from other countries to come here to live.   ☐ ☐ ■

    a. united states
    b. united States
    c. United States

a   b   c

5. These <u>People come</u> here looking for   ☐   ☐   ☐
   opportunities.

   a. People come
   b. People comes
   c. people come

6. <u>Their want</u> to be able to get jobs and attend   ☐   ☐   ☐
   school.

   a. Their want
   b. Their wants
   c. They want

7. <u>They comes</u> from countries like the former   ☐   ☐   ☐
   U.S.S.R, Poland, China, Mexico, and India.

   a. They comes
   b. They come
   c. Them come

8. When they arrive, <u>them have</u> very few   ☐   ☐   ☐
   belongings.

   a. them have
   b. them has
   c. they have

9. One of the first things many <u>immigrants wants</u>   ☐   ☐   ☐
   to do is learn to speak English.

   a. immigrants wants
   b. Immigrants want
   c. immigrants want

10. English <u>are not an easy</u> language to learn.   ☐   ☐   ☐

    a. are not an easy
    b. is not an easily
    c. is not an easy

11. <u>Immigrants have</u> difficulty with the language.   ☐   ☐   ☐

    a. Immigrants have
    b. Immigrants has
    c. Immigrant's have

12. An immigrant has to find a new <u>job housing</u>,   ☐   ☐   ☐
    and friends.

    a. job housing, and
    b. job, housing, and
    c. job housing and

Check your work on page 211.

YOUR TURN TO WRITE
WRITING LETTERS

Take out your writing folder or notebook. You will be writing two short letters for this assignment. One will be a business letter. The other will be a personal letter. Remember to set up both letters properly. They should follow the forms you studied on pages 134–137.

If you like, you can use stationery and mail one or both of the letters. It is also fine to mail letters written on notebook paper.

PUTTING YOUR SKILLS TO WORK

Part 1: The Business Letter

Directions: For this part of the assignment, you are to write a short business letter. You may write to a company about a matter of your choosing, or you may use the following suggestion.

Write a letter requesting a copy of the *Consumer Information Catalog.* Write to S. James, Consumer Information Center, P.O. Box 100, Pueblo, CO 81002. If you mail the letter, the Consumer Information Center will send you this catalog of government publications that might be helpful to you.

Part 2: The Personal Letter

Directions: Write a letter to someone you haven't seen in a long time describing your latest vacation, your house or apartment, your car, or a person in your life right now. In this letter you must use adjectives, adverbs, and items in a series. So, be certain to be as specific as possible with the descriptions.

If you tell about a vacation, you can list the places you stopped and use commas in the list. If you are describing your house, your car, or a person, you can separate the descriptive words with commas.

☑ Writing Checklist

❑ Does your business letter have a return address, a date, an inside address, a greeting, a body, a closing, a signature, and a name?

❑ Does your personal letter have a date, a greeting, a body, a closing, and a signature?

❑ Is the punctuation correct?

❑ Did you use verbs and pronouns correctly?

CHAPTER 7

JOURNAL WRITING
USING YOUR IMAGINATION

If you could be anyone in the world. . . Most people spend time fantasizing. They daydream about the people they would like to be. For some reason the grass always seems greener on the other side of the fence. Another person always seems to have a more enjoyable, more exciting, or more glamorous life.

Does being a champion wrestler, a shift foreman, a glamorous movie star, or a multibillionaire fit your secret fantasy? Does life in the fast lane seem to be calling you, or are you ready to slow down and hibernate in your own warm little spot of the world and watch life from an easy chair?

Here is your chance to think through who or what you have always dreamed about being. Use one of the techniques learned earlier in the book to get your thoughts started. Try clustering or brainstorming. Go back to the beginning of Chapter 2 or Chapter 5 if you want to review one of these methods.

Remember, in your journal, you don't have to worry about using correct grammar and spelling. Just relax and write your own private thoughts for your eyes alone.

JOURNAL ENTRY

Directions: First, put down the name of your desired identity and brainstorm your thoughts about that identity. Then organize your thoughts. After that, write one or more paragraphs on who you would be if you could be anyone in the world.

Remember, when you fantasize, you can be anything you want to be. Get out your journal and start fantasizing. The sky's the limit! You really might make an award-winning television star, the most adept sports car racer in the world, or a great parent.

LANGUAGE SKILLS
COMBINING SENTENCES

COMPOUND SUBJECTS AND COMPOUND PREDICATES

Sentences in which the subjects or predicates have two or more parts will be the topic of this section. You will review compound subjects and work with compound predicates to expand your knowledge of sentence structure.

You have already studied compound subjects. A sentence has a compound subject when the subject is in two or more parts. The following sentences have compound subjects. Each part of the subject in each sentence is in dark type.

> **Ray** and **Ted** have been going to junior college for one year.

> **Their counselors**, **their teachers**, and **their families** want them
> to continue their education.

In each of those sentences, the subjects shared the same predicate. When you have two sentences with the same or very similar information, often you can combine the subjects. For example, the following two sentences can be combined by using a compound subject, like this:

> Ray complained about the cafeteria's food. Ted complained
> about the cafeteria's food.

> **Ray and Ted** complained about the cafeteria's food.

Read the following pair of sentences. Then, on the blank lines, combine them into one sentence with a compound subject.

The dietitian thought they had valid complaints. The cook thought they had valid complaints.

_____

_____

You should have written this sentence: *The dietitian and the cook thought they had valid complaints.*

Compound Predicates

Just as you can combine subjects of sentences with similar or related information, you can combine predicates that have the same subject. When you do this, you have a *compound predicate*. Here are some examples of how two sentences can be combined into one sentence with a compound predicate.

Ted works in the mornings. Ted studies in the evenings.
Ted works in the mornings and studies in the evenings.

Ray belongs to the Spanish Club. He is its treasurer.
Ray belongs to the Spanish Club and is its treasurer.

Now you try combining the following pair of sentences into one sentence with a compound predicate. Both of these sentences are about the prison library. Write the combined sentence on the blank lines.

The library opens early in the morning. It quickly fills with students.

_____

_____

You should have written this sentence: *The library opens early in the morning and quickly fills with students.*

Now try another example. Combine the next two sentences into one sentence with a compound predicate.

Bruce is taking accounting. He hates it.

_____

You should have written this sentence: *Bruce is taking accounting and hates it.*

EXERCISE 1: IDENTIFYING COMPOUND SUBJECTS AND PREDICATES

Directions: Read the following sentences. Decide whether each sentence has a compound subject or compound predicate and underline the compound parts. In the blank, write *CS* if there is a compound subject or *CP* if there is a compound predicate. The first one is done as an example.

  CS   1. The immigrants and their host families met at the airport.

_____ 2. They were happy to see each other and were eager to get acquainted.

_____ 3. American food, clothing, and housing seemed strange to the people from other countries.

_____ 4. Each person was given his own bedroom and was scheduled for English lessons.

Check your work on page 211.

EXERCISE 2: COMPOUNDING SUBJECTS AND PREDICATES

Directions: Using a compound subject or compound predicate, combine the following pairs of sentences. The first one is done as an example.

1. Sharon wrote a letter to her parents during lunch.
   She mailed it on her way home.

   Sharon wrote a letter to her parents during lunch and mailed it on her way home.

2. Sharon planned to visit her parents for Thanksgiving.
   Sharon's brother planned to visit them for Thanksgiving too.

   _____

   _____

3. They were looking forward to seeing their parents.
   They could hardly wait to taste their mother's cooking.

   _____

   _____

4. Sharon was surprised by the answer to her letter.
   Sharon's brother was surprised by the answer.

   _____

   _____

5. Sharon's mother was looking forward to visiting Sharon at
   Thanksgiving. She could hardly wait to taste Sharon's cooking!

   _____

   _____

Check your work on page 211.

USING CONJUNCTIONS TO COMBINE SENTENCES

Sentences that contain related ideas can be combined to make longer, more interesting sentences. The sentences do not have to have the same subject or the same predicate to be combined. Look at the following two short sentences and the combined sentence.

Rosa lost her sewing job. She has no other skills.
Rosa lost her sewing job, **and** she has no other skills.

In that example, both subjects and both predicates are in the new sentence. You can combine two related sentences by keeping both sentences and putting a joining word between them. These joining words are called *conjunctions*.

Here are seven common conjunctions and some examples showing how they are used. Notice that a comma comes before the conjunction in each of the example sentences.

Conjunctions

To add information, use *and*.

>The night was dark and stormy, **and** the lights went out.

To show a contrast, use *but* or *yet*.

>The Laundromat was closed, **but** the manager let me in.
>This coat is thirty years old, **yet** people still admire it.

To show cause, then the effect, use *so*.

>The drain was clogged, **so** Margaret called a plumber.

To show the effect, then the cause, use *for*.

>They got a new kitten, **for** their cat had disappeared.

To show two alternatives, use *or*.

>Either I'll go to the party, **or** I'll stay home and study.

To show two negatives, use *nor*.

>The sun isn't going to come out, **nor** will it rain.

Choosing the Right Conjunction

When you choose a conjunction, you must be careful to choose one that shows how the two thoughts are related. Look at the following example.

>I ran for the bus, **but** I missed it.

The conjunction *but* shows the contrast between the two thoughts. The person did all he could, but he was not able to reach the bus in time. If he had written, "I ran for the bus, *so* I missed it," the sentence wouldn't make sense.

Now look at another example. Notice the conjunction *and*.

>Tina joined an aerobics class, and she loves exercising.

Those two thoughts can be joined logically by a comma and the conjunction *and*. You would not say, "Tina joined an aerobics class, *but* she loves exercising." That would make it sound as though aerobics were not exercising.

Read the following sentence. Choose the best conjunction (*and, or, for, nor, so, but,* or *yet*) and write it in the blank between the two complete thoughts.

Ed wants to exercise more, _____ he is joining a health club.

Did you choose *so*? If you did, you realized that the first thought is the cause and the second thought is the effect.

Try another example. Choose the best conjunction and write it in the blank.

Start helping with chores around the house, _____ you will have to move out.

Did you choose *or*? The two thoughts are alternatives—either one or the other will happen.

Don't Overuse Commas

As you have seen, when you join two complete thoughts with a conjunction, a comma comes before the conjunction. You use a comma before a conjunction only when you join two complete thoughts. Remember that a complete thought has *both* a subject and a verb. Here are two sentences that do not contain two complete thoughts. Instead, they have compound predicates.

I ran for the bus **but** missed it.

The second part of the compound predicate, *missed it*, is not a complete thought, so no comma is used before *but*.

Tina joined an aerobics class **and** loves exercising.

The second part of the compound predicate, *loves exercising*, is not a complete thought, so no comma is used before *and*.

Three sentences follow. Only one of them has a conjunction combining two complete thoughts. Find that sentence and put the comma in the correct place.

The car broke down on the highway and Sam had it towed.
The car broke down on the highway but started up again right
    away.
The car broke down on the highway and was towed.

Did you place your comma in the first sentence after *highway*? The second and third sentences do not have two complete thoughts, so you do not need to add a comma.

EXERCISE 3: PRACTICING WITH CONJUNCTIONS
AND COMMAS

Directions: Circle the conjunction in each of these sentences and add commas in the correct places. Each of these sentences contains two complete thoughts. The first one is done as an example.

1. Thrift stores are great places to shop, (and) they have many bargains.

2. Some of the customers who visit them have very little money but others just want to find a good buy.

3. Nice clothes sell quickly so smart customers shop on the day new items are stocked.

4. Men and women go to these stores for clothes but children like to look for toys.

5. Some shops are open at odd hours yet shoppers fill the aisles.

6. Furniture is very inexpensive for it has been used.

7. Many items seem in bad shape yet they can be beautiful when repaired.

Check your work on page 212.

EXERCISE 4: COMBINING SENTENCES

Directions: Rewrite the following sentences. Add a conjunction and a comma to each set of sentences to form one combined sentence. The first one is done as an example.

and   but   yet   so   or

1. Children are fun. Many people enjoy working with them.

   Children are fun, and many people enjoy working with them.

2. Horses are farm animals. People keep them in cities.

   _____

   _____

3. Drugs are a serious problem. Many teenagers think they are harmless.

_____

_____

4. Danita needed a new dress. She went shopping this morning.

_____

_____

5. His team has to win this game. Bob will lose his bet.

_____

_____

Check your work on page 212.

PUTTING YOUR SKILLS TO WORK

Directions: You just completed an exercise in which you added commas and conjunctions to sentences that someone else had written. Now you will use your own thoughts to write combined sentences. In this exercise, write carefully and correctly, using all the skills you have learned to help you write good sentences.

Write two short related sentences on each of the following subjects: food, friends, clothes. (Or you may pick three topics of your choosing.) First write the short sentences and then rewrite them using a comma and a conjunction to join them. Remember, the conjunctions are _and, but, or, nor, for, so,_ and _yet._

Here is a sample for you to follow.

> Hot chocolate is a great drink. It has hundreds of calories.
> Hot chocolate is a great drink, but it has hundreds of calories.

Write your sentences in your writing folder or notebook and remember to date your work. You will have three sets of sentences that are not combined, and you will have three combined sentences.

☑ _Writing Checklist_

❏ Does each of your combined sentences have a comma before the conjunction?

❏ Does each combined sentence have two complete thoughts?

❏ Have you chosen a conjunction that shows how your thoughts are related?

USING CONNECTORS

Connectors are another group of joining words you can use to combine sentences.

Some common connectors are listed below. Each one has a specific meaning.

Connectors

To show contrast, use *however, nevertheless,* or *instead.*

  Brad wants to be a team player; **however**, he loves glory.
  Anita was grounded; **nevertheless**, she went out.
  Yim wanted to go to school; **instead**, she got a job.

To add more information, use *furthermore* or *moreover.*

  You are a good friend; **furthermore**, you are my best friend.
  Martin wants to help; **moreover**, he insists on washing the dishes.

To show a cause, then its effect, use *therefore* or *consequently.*

  We love children; **therefore**, we adopted six of them.
  Alan enters every contest he can; **consequently**, he often wins.

Punctuating Connectors

Notice that there is a semicolon (;) in front of each connector and a comma after it in each of the sample sentences. Study the following sentences. Circle the connector in each sentence and add semicolons and commas where needed. The first one is done for you.

Todd's chair broke yesterday; (therefore) he has to fix it.

Rhonda hurried otherwise she would be late for work.

Amy is 87 today furthermore she intends to live to be 107.

Life is crazy nevertheless I love it.

Did you circle *otherwise, furthermore,* and *nevertheless*? They are the connectors, and each one should have a semicolon in front of it and a comma following it. All the other words are part of the two related thoughts.

Choosing the Right Connector

Always be careful to choose a connector that shows the relationship between the thoughts in the combined sentence. Look at this example. Why is *consequently* used in the combined sentence?

> Maria went to secretarial school. She got a better job.
> Maria went to secretarial school; **consequently**, she got a
>   better job.

Consequently is used in the combined sentence because it shows that the better job was a *result* of Maria's additional schooling.

Here is another example. How does *therefore* show the relationship between the two thoughts?

> The men like weightlifting; **therefore**, they often go to the gym.

In that sentence, *therefore* is used to show that going to the gym is the *effect* of the men's liking weightlifting.

Now you try. What connector would work well in this sentence? (You can look back at the connectors in the box on page 151.) Write a logical connector in the blank.

> Steve needs a new car; _____, he has no money.

Did you write *however*? It shows the *contrast* between needing a new car and not having the money to buy one.

Try another example. Read the following sentence and think about how the two thoughts are related. Write a connector that makes sense in the blank.

> The car's brakes are worn; _____, the body is
> badly rusted.

In that sentence, *moreover* or *furthermore* should be used to show that the second thought *adds information* to the first.

EXERCISE 5: CORRECTING SENTENCES WITH CONNECTORS

Directions: In this exercise, a part of each sentence is underlined. After the sentence, you will find three possible ways to write the underlined section. The first option is always the same as the underlined part of the sentence. Choose the option that makes the sentence correct and fill in the box under **a**, **b**, or **c** to indicate your answer. The first one is done as an example.

	a	b	c

1. Kenny has played the banjo since he was <u>three, instead; he</u> is the best banjo picker in town.

    a. three, instead; he
    b. three; consequently, he
    c. three, consequently; he

2. The auto industry offers high-paying <u>jobs; therefore, applications</u> have increased.

    a. jobs; therefore, applications
    b. jobs; therefore; applications
    c. jobs, therefore, applications

3. I frequently lose my house <u>keys; therefore,</u> I lock my car keys in my car at least once a week.

    a. keys; therefore, I
    b. keys; furthermore, I
    c. keys, furthermore; I

4. For some of the armed services, a diploma is <u>required, however; not</u> all branches have this requirement.

    a. required, however; not
    b. required; however, not
    c. required; however not

5. Phillip hoped to win a million in the magazine <u>sweepstakes; instead he</u> won five tubes of lipstick.

    a. sweepstakes; instead he
    b. sweepstakes, instead he,
    c. sweepstakes; instead, he

6. Entry-level jobs are <u>plentiful; therefore; young</u> people can find work if they aren't picky.

    a. plentiful; therefore; young
    b. plentiful, therefore; young
    c. plentiful; therefore, young

                                                    a   b   c

7. Sarah is really <u>bright moreover; she</u> always puts   ☐   ☐   ☐
   herself down.

   a. bright moreover; she
   b. bright; nevertheless, she
   c. bright; moreover, she

8. Some people are true basketball <u>fanatics, however</u>   ☐   ☐   ☐
   <u>others</u> are wild about hockey.

   a. fanatics, however others
   b. fanatics therefore; others
   c. fanatics; however, others

Check your work on page 212.

EXERCISE 6: WRITING SENTENCES WITH CONNECTORS

Directions: Join the following sentences using connectors. Remember that
the connector that you use has to make sense. Be certain to put the correct
punctuation in each sentence.

      therefore   nevertheless   furthermore   consequently
      moreover   however   instead

1. The house is a mess. It must be cleaned.

   _____

   _____

2. The police searched the neighborhood for drugs. They vowed to jail
   all dealers.

   _____

   _____

3. After the race, the drivers were exhausted. They went to the party.

   _____

   _____

4. The Joneses were evicted from their apartment. Mr. Jones lost his job.

   _____

   _____

5. Dorothy thought she would get a small raise. She was surprised with a ten percent salary increase.

    _____

    _____

6. Mom asked me to get orange juice. I got grape juice.

    _____

    _____

7. Electric heat is very expensive. We keep the thermostats turned down to 65 degrees.

    _____

    _____

Check your work on page 212.

PUTTING YOUR SKILLS TO WORK

Directions: Take out your writing folder or notebook. You are to write three sentences using connectors. Use any three of these words: *consequently, furthermore, however, instead, moreover, nevertheless,* and *therefore.* These words must join two related thoughts. Write carefully and correctly, using all the skills you have been practicing for writing good sentences.

You can use your own ideas; however, if you need suggestions, choose from the following ideas: your family, an accident, your best friend, television, or exercise.

After writing the sentences, circle the connectors and underline the complete thoughts.

☑ *Writing Checklist*

❑ Do you have two complete thoughts in each sentence?

❑ Is there a semicolon before each connector?

❑ Is there a comma following each connector?

❑ Did you use a connector that makes sense in your sentence?

USING SUBORDINATING CONJUNCTIONS

Often you will be able to combine sentences by using another group of conjunctions that show cause, contrast, condition, or time. When these words are used, one part of the sentence becomes dependent on the other part to make sense. Here is a list of some *subordinating conjunctions* and examples showing how they are used.

Subordinating Conjunctions

To show cause and effect, use *because* or *since*.

> **Because** she couldn't dance, Sandra stayed home.
> Peter took the job **since** the pay was good.

To show contrast, use *though* or *although*.

> **Though** Harry was elected, he doesn't feel victorious.
> The Bennets rented the apartment **although** it was too small.

To show condition, use *if*.

> **If** Blair gets home on time, we will go to the game.

To show time, use *when, after,* or *before*.

> **When** the cows come home, Gretna will milk them.
> **After** she milks the cows, Jerry will feed them.
> Kenton will sample the milk **before** Kimmy scrubs the milkhouse.

If the subordinating conjunction is the first word in the sentence, place a comma between the two ideas. If the subordinating conjunction is in the middle of the sentence, you should not use a comma. Study the sample sentences in the box to see this pattern.

Now practice using the subordinating conjunctions. The following examples show how to combine two sentences using these conjunctions.

Because and *since* join a cause to an effect.

> Sam had no money. He couldn't buy a soda.
> **Because** Sam had no money, he couldn't buy a soda.

> I refuse to go to that store. Everything there is overpriced.
> I refuse to go to that store **since** everything there is overpriced.

Use *because* or *since* to combine the two following sentences. *Because* or *since* must be attached to the cause. Write the combined sentence on the line below.

> Elsie sliced the roast carelessly. She cut her hand.

_____

You could have written one of the following answers:

> Since Elsie sliced the roast carelessly, she cut her hand.
> Elsie cut her hand because she sliced the roast carelessly.

Though and *although* show a contradiction between two ideas.

> Running in marathons is exhausting. I enjoy it.
> **Though** running in marathons is exhausting, I enjoy it.

> Herman took the job. It meant a huge salary cut.
> Herman took the job **although** it meant a huge salary cut.

Use *though* or *although* to combine the following two sentences. Write the combined sentence on the blank line.

> Bob had twenty-six shirts. He insisted he needed more.

The correct combined sentence could read like this:

> Though Bob had twenty-six shirts, he insisted he needed more.

If shows a condition and a result. If one thing happens, another thing will happen. *If* is attached to the condition.

> **If** the weather is good, we will go swimming tomorrow.

Join the following sentences using *if* to show a conditional relationship. Write the combined sentence on the blank line.

> The baby wakes up by 8:30 A.M. We can go to the park.

You could have combined these sentences in two ways:

> If the baby wakes up by 8:30 A.M., we can go to the park.
> We can go to the park if the baby wakes up by 8:30 A.M.

When, *after*, and *before* are time words. *When* shows that two actions are taking place at the same time. *After* and *before* show the order of two actions. By using them, you can tell your reader which action came first.

When you do the dishes, I'll vacuum the floor.
After you do the dishes, I'll vacuum the floor.
I'll vacuum the floor **before** you do the dishes.

Combine the following sentences to show proper time order. Use *when* to show that both things are done at the same time.

Tina goes out with her friends. Ed takes care of the baby.

_____

You should have written this answer: *When Tina goes out with her friends, Ed takes care of the baby.*

EXERCISE 7: COMPLETING SENTENCES WITH SUBORDINATING CONJUNCTIONS

Directions: Fill in the blanks in the following sentences with one of the subordinating conjunctions from the list below. More than one of the conjunctions will work in some sentences. The first one is done as an example.

because	though	if	after
since	although	when	before

1. Bruno will go to work today _____*if*_____ he is feeling better.

2. _____ the examination was over, the doctor wrote the report.

3. Fast food restaurants like to hire adults _____ adults are more dependable workers.

4. Doris bought the plate _____ it completed her china set.

5. _____ Bob had retired, his employer asked him to return to work.

6. _____ I finish this assignment by tomorrow, I can take Friday off.

Check your work on page 212.

EXERCISE 8: WRITING SENTENCES WITH SUBORDINATING CONJUNCTIONS

Directions: Combine each pair of sentences, using one of the subordinating conjunctions in **dark type**. If the conjunction starts with a capital letter, put it at the beginning of the sentence. Be sure to punctuate your sentences correctly. The first one is done as an example.

When   because   Though   Before   if   Since   after   although

1. David gets home. We will show him the pictures.

   When David gets home, we will show him the pictures.

2. I save money on bus fare. I ride my bike to work every day.

3. Chan went to the doctor yesterday. She doesn't feel any better today.

4. The Jellybeans recorded their first big hit in 1964. They were completely unknown.

5. The police will be able to arrest the drug dealer. Maura can identify him in a lineup.

6. Margaret mowed the lawn. Greg agreed to do the raking.

7. Allison will earn more money. She graduates from high school.

8. Jenka gave me the money. She needed it herself.

Check your work on pages 212–213.

PUTTING YOUR SKILLS TO WORK

Directions: This assignment is for your writing folder or notebook. Put the date at the top of your paper. Write carefully and correctly, using your skills for writing sentences. Write five sentences using the subordinating conjunctions. Use any five of the following conjunctions:

because	if
since	when
though	after
although	before

These words must combine two related ideas in a way that makes sense. You can use your own ideas in the sentences. If you need suggestions, write sentences about these topics: your city, your neighborhood, your vacation, your home.

☑ *Writing Checklist*

❏ Did you combine two ideas in each of your sentences?

❏ If a sentence started with a subordinating conjunction, did you separate the two ideas with a comma?

❏ If a subordinating conjunction came in the middle of a sentence, did you remember not to separate the ideas with a comma?

PUNCTUATING PERFECTLY

REVIEW OF COMMAS AND SEMICOLONS IN COMBINED SENTENCES

You have been learning to combine related sentences by using three types of joining words. When you used conjunctions like *and, but, or,* and *yet,* you placed a comma in front of the conjunction.

Loretta pushed down the brake pedal, **but** the truck didn't stop.

When you used connectors like *however, nevertheless, consequently,* and *moreover,* you placed a semicolon in front of the connector and a comma after it.

Loretta pushed down the brake pedal; **however,** the truck didn't stop.

Then you used subordinating conjunctions like *because*, *though*, *if*, and *after*. You separated the two thoughts with a comma if the sentence began with a subordinating conjunction. If the subordinating conjunction came in the middle of the sentence, you didn't use a comma.

> The truck roared down the hill **because** its brakes failed.
> **Because** its brakes failed, the truck roared down the hill.

EXERCISE 9: PRACTICING PUNCTUATION

Directions: Add the correct punctuation to each of the following sentences. You will be punctuating all the different kinds of sentences you have studied in this chapter. The first one is done as an example.

1. Being new in town is not easy; however, there are many

   support groups.

2. Churches form newcomers groups and community agencies do the same thing.

3. Many families are nervous about going to meetings but they can learn to look forward to them.

4. People go to the meetings because they want to make new friends.

5. Some girls feel that they will appear to be looking for boys consequently they won't attend these meetings.

6. Many boys fear that same thing so they stay home too.

7. Others are more optimistic therefore they go to meet people of both sexes.

8. When people have interests in common they may develop good relationships.

9. Very vain people don't go to see who is there instead they go to be seen.

10. The types of people who attend meetings vary furthermore the reasons they attend are quite varied.

Check your work on page 213.

EXERCISE 10: CHAPTER REVIEW
Part 1

To complete this part of the review, you will use the information studied in this chapter, including the material on combining sentences. First answer as many questions as possible without looking back in the chapter. Then go back through the chapter to complete any remaining answers.

Directions: Read the following sentences. Then combine them, as directed, in three different ways.

Getting up for work is not easy. I am usually late.

1. Use *so* with a comma to combine the two sentences.

_____

2. Use a semicolon with *therefore* to combine the two sentences.

_____

3. Use *Because* and a comma to combine the two sentences.

_____

Directions: The underlined parts of the following sentences may contain errors. Select the choice that makes each sentence correct. The first choice will always be the same as the underlined part.

	a	b	c

4. Farsighted adults plan for <u>retirement; and they</u> hope   ☐ ☐ ☐
   to spend many years enjoying themselves.

   a. retirement; and they
   b. retirement, and they
   c. retirement; and, they

5. Workers try to save <u>money, furthermore some</u>   ☐ ☐ ☐
   businesses offer excellent payroll deduction plans.

   a. money, furthermore some
   b. money; furthermore, some
   c. money; furthermore some

6. Companies have high <u>profits, and employees</u>   ☐ ☐ ☐
   sometimes get their share of them.

   a. profits, and employees
   b. profits, or employees
   c. profits nor employees

a   b   c

☐   ☐   ☐

7. They offer profit-sharing <u>plans; consequently the</u> employees feel they are a part of the company.

   a. plans; consequently the
   b. plans; consequently, the
   c. plans, consequently, the

☐   ☐   ☐

8. It is helpful to have <u>savings; instead,</u> you reach retirement age.

   a. savings; instead, you
   b. savings; furthermore, you
   c. savings when you

☐   ☐   ☐

9. Unfortunately, it is not always possible to save <u>earnings because</u> they are needed to pay bills.

   a. earnings because
   b. earnings; because
   c. earnings. Because

☐   ☐   ☐

10. Social Security benefits offer <u>income, but</u> some added funds help.

   a. income, but
   b. income but
   c. income; but

Part 2

To complete this section of the review, you will need to use all the information that you have studied so far in this book.

Directions: Complete the following.

1. Name the four types of sentences and tell what kind of endmark each one takes.

   _____

   _____

   _____

2. What are compound subjects? _____

   _____

Directions: Find the mistake in each of the following sentences and fill in the box that corresponds to the letter of the mistake. The first one is done for you.

	a	b	c

3. Peanut <u>butter</u>, one of America's favorite <u>foods</u>, <u>are</u>
   _a   _b   _c

   high in protein.

☐ ☐ ■

4. The nutritionist <u>said</u>, "<u>Stress</u> can be relieved with
   _a   _b

   vitamin $B_{12.}$
          _c

☐ ☐ ☐

5. The team members <u>is</u> negotiating <u>their</u> contracts in
   _a   _b

   closed individual <u>sessions</u>.
                     _c

☐ ☐ ☐

6. The <u>students</u> or the teacher <u>are</u> in charge of the
   _a   _b

   <u>report</u>.
   _c

☐ ☐ ☐

7. <u>Her</u> planned to purchase <u>chips</u>, <u>pretzels</u>, and dip for
   _a   _b   _c

   the party.

☐ ☐ ☐

8. The <u>womens'</u> support group <u>meets</u> every
   _a   _b

   <u>Wednesday</u>.
   _c

☐ ☐ ☐

9. <u>Dad</u>, when <u>are</u> the guests <u>coming.</u>
   _a   _b   _c

☐ ☐ ☐

10. The <u>hungry</u> man <u>ate</u> his dinner <u>hurried</u>.
    _a   _b   _c

☐ ☐ ☐

Check your work on page 213.

YOUR TURN TO WRITE
WRITING A PARAGRAPH

Take out your writing notebook or folder again. Remember to date the assignment. This time you are going to write a paragraph on a consumer issue or a current event. Pick one of the following topics:

- A wise car buyer shops around.
- It's best to buy clothes out of season.
- Vote for _____!
- Join the campaign to stop hunger.
- Drugs are everyone's problem.
- Your choice

PUTTING YOUR SKILLS TO WORK

Directions: Choose a topic that you can relate to and tell why you feel the way you do. Write a paragraph using short sentences. Write at least eight sentences. Then try to combine some of the sentences in your paragraph, using the sentence-combining techniques you have been learning in this chapter. Use the charts on pages 147, 151, and 156 to help you choose good joining words. Write carefully and correctly so that others will understand your writing.

Here is a sample from part of a paragraph on voting for a favorite candidate. The first paragraph began as follows:

> Vote for Olga for mayor. She is the best candidate. She has lived here all her life. Olga knows our town very well. She is a Democrat. She gets along with Republicans. . . .

Now look at the same paragraph with combined sentences.

> Vote for Olga for mayor because she is the best candidate. She has lived here all her life and knows our town very well. She is a Democrat; however, she gets along with Republicans. . . .

If you spend enough time working on your paragraph to develop it thoroughly, the sentences will relate to each other, and you will be able to combine them easily.

Pick your topic and begin writing.

☑ Writing Checklist

❏ Do you have at least eight sentences in your paragraph?

❏ Have you used sentence-combining methods correctly?

❏ Have you combined sentences so that their relationship is clear?

CHAPTER 8

JOURNAL WRITING
TODAY'S CONCERNS OR YESTERDAY'S MEMORIES?

Some people spend much of their time thinking about current concerns. Others are caught up in things that happened to them in the past. This journal entry will give you an opportunity to work through one of those two themes. You may use any technique you like to start writing. Pick a good topic—one of your current concerns or one of your memories of the past.

If you are writing about your current concerns, would you like to see a woman president? Do you believe that war could be outlawed? Would you like to see the government train people on welfare for new jobs? Perhaps your concerns are more personal. Do people who comment on the way you walk irritate you? Are you worried about your family? Would you like to tell your neighbors how much you appreciate them? Here's an opportunity to speak your piece.

Maybe you would rather write about the past. Write about your favorite childhood memory or another event from your past. Was there a special birthday celebration? Did someone surprise you with a visit? Were you the class clown in elementary school? Did you hit the home run that won the Little League championship?

JOURNAL ENTRY

Directions: Decide on a topic. Use one of the suggestions above or a topic of your own. Cluster, brainstorm, or just write everything you can about the topic. Enjoy saying what's on your mind or reliving a memory. Remember, in your journal, you don't have to worry about correct grammar and spelling. You are just writing for yourself.

LANGUAGE SKILLS
NEW TOPICS IN SENTENCE STRUCTURE

Just as an automobile will not run if it is not put together correctly, a sentence cannot be understood if it is not put together correctly. In the last chapter, you learned how to combine whole sentences with joining words. In this chapter, you will be practicing two new ways to put ideas together correctly by using describing phrases and parallel structure. Using these techniques will help to make your sentences more interesting.

USING DESCRIBING PHRASES CORRECTLY

A describing phrase can tell you something about a noun or a pronoun. You worked on subject-verb agreement with describing phrases in Chapter 5, so you have seen examples of them. In this chapter, you'll learn more about writing sentences with describing phrases.

Describing phrases must always be placed as close as possible to the word they describe. Here's an example:

> Mona entered the office at midnight. She was carrying the
>   stolen papers.
> **Carrying the stolen papers**, Mona entered the office at midnight.

In the combined sentence, the describing phrase *Carrying the stolen papers* tells you something about *Mona*. Therefore, that phrase is placed next to *Mona*.

A describing phrase is **misplaced** if it is not placed next to the noun or pronoun it describes. Here is an example of a sentence with a misplaced describing phrase:

The cowboy entered the saloon wearing matching pistols.

The describing phrase, *wearing matching pistols*, is placed next to *saloon*. The wording of the sentence tells you that the saloon was wearing matching pistols! But your common sense tells you that the cowboy must be wearing them. The sentence could be rewritten clearly in either of the following two ways:

Wearing matching pistols, the cowboy entered the saloon.
The cowboy **wearing matching pistols** entered the saloon.

In both of those examples, the describing phrase *wearing matching pistols* is next to *cowboy*, the word it describes.

Here are two examples of what happens when describing phrases are misplaced. Look at the pictures and read the sentences below them.

Mr. Brown purchased the coat from the saleswoman that cost $100.

We watched the batter hit a home run from box seats.

Of course, it must be the coat that costs $100, not the saleswoman. Your common sense tells you that the batter is not hitting a home run from box seats.

Here are the sentences rewritten correctly. The describing phrases, which are in **dark type**, are placed next to the words they describe, which are underlined.

Mr. Brown purchased the <u>coat</u> **that cost $100** from the saleswoman.

From box seats, <u>we</u> watched the batter hit a home run.

Three sentences follow. A describing phrase to insert in each sentence is also given. First underline the word that the phrase describes. Then rewrite the sentences, placing each describing phrase as close as possible to the word it should describe. The first one is done for you.

Please put the <u>presents</u> under the tree. *(that you wrapped)*

Please put the presents that you wrapped under the tree.

Albert saw a dog chasing a cat. *(walking to work)*

_____

Danny put the ring on Carmen's finger. *(worn by his grandmother)*

_____

Did you rewrite the sentences like this?

> **Walking to work,** <u>Albert</u> saw a dog chasing a cat.
> Danny put the <u>ring</u> **worn by his grandmother** on Carmen's finger.

EXERCISE 1: IDENTIFYING MISPLACED DESCRIBING PHRASES

Directions: Read the following sentences. Circle the letter of the sentence in each pair that is written correctly. In each correct sentence, underline the describing phrase and circle the word it describes. The first one is done as an example.

1. (a.) The (woman) <u>in purple shoes</u> caught the Frisbee.
   b. The woman caught the Frisbee in purple shoes.

2. a. The desk that is 500 years old was bought in an antique shop near Chicago.
   b. The desk was bought in an antique shop near Chicago that is 500 years old.

3. a. Clay left on the train wearing a sailor's cap.
   b. Wearing a sailor's cap, Clay left on the train.

4. a. The people yawned through the movie sitting in the front row.
   b. The people sitting in the front row yawned through the movie.

5. a. Climbing to the top of the mountain, we saw the pine trees.
   b. We saw the pine trees climbing to the top of the mountain.

Check your work on page 213.

EXERCISE 2: WRITING SENTENCES WITH DESCRIBING PHRASES

Directions: Insert the describing phrase into each of the following sentences. Be sure to place the phrase next to the word it describes. The first one is done as an example.

1. He let the puppy out. *(wearing only his pajamas and slippers)*

   Wearing only his pajamas and slippers, he let the puppy out.

2. Luke noticed the unusual painting. *(hanging on the wall)*

   _____

3. The actors were getting ready to face the audience. *(in their dressing rooms)*

   _____

4. The salesman handed the slacks to Geraldine. *(with the red stripes)*

_____

5. The team fumbled the ball in the second half. *(in blue uniforms)*

_____

6. The boy gave me change for a dollar. *(selling newspapers)*

_____

Check your work on pages 213–214.

PARALLEL STRUCTURE

When writing sentences, you need to use parallel structure to list more than one thing or idea. *Parallel structure* means that items are in the same form. Here is an example that shows parallel structure:

John likes **fishing** and **boating**.

The words *fishing* and *boating* both end in *ing*. The same forms are used. You would not want to write this sentence:

John likes to fish and boating.

That sentence is incorrect because the forms of the two items are different: *to fish* and *boating*. However, you could write this sentence:

John likes **to fish** and **to boat**.

Here's another example of a sentence with correct parallel structure. Notice that the three parts of the list are all adjectives.

The cartoon was **funny**, **short**, and **unusual**.

The words *funny*, *short*, and *unusual* are all adjectives that describe *cartoon*. You would not want to write this sentence:

The cartoon was funny, short, and was unusual.

That sentence is incorrect because the third part of the list now contains a verb *(was)* instead of just an adjective.

Here's a sentence that contains longer parallel parts. Underline the two phrases that are in parallel form.

> The employer promised to increase salaries and give more coffee breaks.

The two phrases are *increase salaries* and *give more coffee breaks*. Both phrases begin with a verb in the same form. You would not want to write this sentence:

> The employer promised to increase salaries and giving more coffee breaks.

That sentence is incorrect because two different verb forms are used, *increase* and *giving*.

One of the following sentences has correct parallel structure. The other two do not. Rewrite each incorrect sentence so that each has parallel structure.

> When he was twenty-one, Richard loved dancing, skiing, and to swim.
> Dorothy is going to school and learning to write.
> Singing in a rock group and to star in a movie are Claude's goals.

_____

_____

_____

You should have rewritten the first sentence. Here are two correct ways to write it:

> When he was twenty-one, Richard loved dancing, skiing, and swimming.
> When he was twenty-one, Richard loved to dance, to ski, and to swim.

You should also have rewritten the third sentence. Here are two correct ways to write it:

> Singing in a rock group and starring in a movie are Claude's goals.
> To sing in a rock group and to star in a movie are Claude's goals.

To correct a sentence that does not have parallel structure, you usually can find more than one possible form. Your goal is to choose one form for the parallel parts and follow through with that form.

EXERCISE 3: IDENTIFYING CORRECT PARALLEL STRUCTURE

Directions: Circle the letter of the sentence that has correct parallel structure in each pair below. Underline the parallel parts in the correct sentence. The first one is done as an example.

1. a. Harold loves working, playing, and to watch good movies.
   b. Harold loves <u>working, playing,</u> and <u>watching good movies</u>.

2. a. Burt can't decide if he wants to be a policeman, a paramedic, or a firefighter.
   b. Burt can't decide if he wants to be a policeman, a paramedic, or work for the fire department.

3. a. Alice plans to polish the silver, to dust the floors, and on washing the clothes.
   b. Alice plans to polish the silver, dust the floors, and wash the clothes.

4. a. Mary Jo draws exquisitely and painting superbly.
   b. Mary Jo draws exquisitely and paints superbly.

5. a. Ronnie's car always stalls out and is leaving him stranded.
   b. Ronnie's car always stalls out and leaves him stranded.

6. a. He wants to build bridges and sell buildings.
   b. He wants to build bridges and selling buildings.

Check your work on page 214.

EXERCISE 4: CORRECTING PARALLEL STRUCTURE

Directions: The following sentences contain errors in parallel structure. Rewrite each sentence with correct parallel structure.

1. Homer went to Texas, got a job, built a house, and he got married.

   _____

2. Getting rich and to buy a car are Dorothy's only interests.

   _____

3. Mystery stories have intrigue, excitement, and full of suspense.

   _____

4. My cousins like to go to the movies, watch television, and then they do weird things to their hair.

   _____

5. Hiram's job requires him to drive many miles and talking to a lot of people.

_____

6. Wendy works very hard but is having fun too.

_____

Check your work on page 214.

LANGUAGE SKILLS
PERFECTING PARAGRAPHS

MATCHING VERBS IN A PARAGRAPH

If you think back to Chapter 4, you may remember that verb tenses show how things happen in time. You studied past, present, and future tenses. When you are writing, you must be certain that the verbs in a paragraph all show the time element of that paragraph.

A paragraph about a past event should use verbs that show the actions took place in the past. Here is an example:

> Mardi **won** first prize in the cooking contest. She **baked** a shoofly pie. It **looked** scrumptious. The Iowa State Fair judges **thought** it **was** delectable.

Notice that every verb in that paragraph is written in the past tense. That tells you that everything happened in the past.

The next example is a paragraph about something taking place in the present. It is written in the present tense.

> The bus **is** very dependable. It **arrives** on time every morning. In bad weather, the driver **drives** cautiously and **gets** all the passengers to work on time.

All the verbs in that paragraph were written in the present tense. They show that this information is true in the present.

Finally, look at a paragraph written in the future tense. The events in this paragraph have not yet taken place.

> There **will be** a severe blizzard tonight. Cars **will have** trouble staying on the highways. Pipes **will freeze**. Power lines **will break**. Snow emergency plans **will go** into effect. The storm **will cause** many problems.

Since that paragraph was written with future-tense verbs, each verb had the word *will* in front of it.

When you are writing, be careful not to shift tenses unnecessarily. For example, you would not want to write these sentences:

> There will be a blizzard tonight. The storm caused many problems.

The second sentence shifted from the future to the past tense. This shift makes the reader wonder whether the storm has already happened or not. As a result, neither sentence makes any sense.

The following paragraph should be written in the past tense. Cross out any verbs that are not written in the past tense and change them to the past tense.

> Albert bought a car phone after he saw mine. He had it put into his car, but he didn't like it. After an hour, he removes it and took it back. The shop owner refuses to refund Albert's money but gave him a store credit.

You should have changed *removes* to *removed* and *refuses* to *refused*.

EXERCISE 5: CHECKING VERB TENSE IN A PARAGRAPH

Directions: Read the following paragraphs. Cross out any verb that is written in an incorrect tense and write the correct tense above it. The new verb should be in the same tense as the other verbs in the paragraph.

Paragraph 1

Glenn loves being outdoors in the Wyoming mountains. He feels close to nature. He was a careful camper. Glenn sets up perfect campsites.

Paragraph 2

A log cabin is his dream. He plans to build one next fall. Plans included a large fieldstone fireplace. Cedar logs are being sent for the shell.

Paragraph 3

The cabin will have only one big room, and it had a bathroom. It will be furnished very sparsely. Glenn will live in the cabin all year round.

Paragraph 4

A herd of deer lived close to the building spot. They left once the land was cleared. They move to a new home close to a nearby stream.

Check your work on page 214.

PARAGRAPH STRUCTURE

You have written many paragraphs while working in this book. As you continue writing, you will want to begin checking each paragraph to make sure that it has a topic sentence and that all the other sentences support that topic.

> The *topic sentence* expresses the main idea of the paragraph. It focuses your writing into one specific area. The *supporting sentences* give details that explain the topic sentence.

For example, you might decide that you would like to write a paragraph on insurance. However, that is a very broad topic. There are life insurance, health insurance, car insurance, home insurance, and many other kinds of insurance.

So you can narrow your topic by deciding to write on life insurance. That is still a broad topic. It can be narrowed even more. You might decide to write about good reasons to purchase life insurance.

That topic can become a very good topic sentence. It makes the purpose of your paragraph very specific. If you wrote the paragraph, you would include only good reasons for buying life insurance. That paragraph might look like this (the topic sentence is in dark type):

> **There are three good reasons for buying life insurance.** First, it gives security to your family in case you die. Second, it can give you retirement income. Finally, you can borrow against the policy if you need a loan.

As you can see, if you have a clear topic sentence, it is easy to write a well-organized paragraph. The topic sentence in that paragraph makes it very clear that everything in the paragraph is about good reasons for buying life insurance.

Whenever you write a paragraph, be certain that all the information you include supports the topic sentence. You would not want to include a sentence like *Life insurance is very expensive* in the paragraph above. The cost of life insurance is not related to the topic sentence.

Read the following paragraph. Find the topic sentence and underline it. One sentence in the paragraph does not belong because it does not support the topic sentence. Cross out the sentence that does not belong.

> Riding subways takes a great deal of knowledge. The passengers must know how to read train schedules. They must know where the station platforms are located. Eating candy helps brighten up a long ride. They must know whether to get off at the front or back of the train.

The first sentence is the topic sentence. The sentence about eating candy does not belong in the paragraph. When a paragraph has a clear topic sentence, it is easy to spot a sentence that is off the topic.

EXERCISE 6: KNOWING THE TOPIC OF A PARAGRAPH

Directions: Six paragraphs are included in this exercise. Read each paragraph and underline the topic sentence—the sentence that tells the main idea of the paragraph. Then cross out the one sentence in each paragraph that does not support the topic sentence. The first one is done as an example.

Paragraph 1

There are several steps to follow when applying for a job. First, contact the company's personnel office to arrange an interview. Second, arrive for the interview five minutes early. ~~Meeting a friend for lunch makes the day more enjoyable~~. Third, accurately complete the employment application. Fourth, be polite when interviewed and answer all questions completely and honestly. Fifth, when the interview is over, thank the person who conducted the interview. Finally, before the day is over, write a thank you note to the interviewer and restate a desire to work for that company.

Paragraph 2

Credit cards are convenient, but they can cost large sums of money. Department stores, gasoline stations, banks, and even telephone companies offer credit as a way to encourage spending. Card holders pay interest on the amount they don't pay off each month. Most cards charge interest rates of 17% to 20% or more. Some cards, such as department store cards and gasoline cards, are used to buy items at a specific place.

Paragraph 3

Caring for an infant is very demanding. An infant must be fed many times each day. His or her diapers must be changed several times a day. They are so cute and so much fun to watch. Often the baby needs care in the middle of the night. Once a baby arrives, parents find their time is not their own.

Paragraph 4

Avid television sports fans are called "armchair athletes." These armchair athletes get their exercise walking from the armchair to the refrigerator and back. They build biceps by crushing soda or beer cans and by changing channels. Soda is better for them because it doesn't contain alcohol. These people spend great amounts of energy cheering or booing the teams on the screen.

Paragraph 5

Three things come together to make a good mystery story. First, the characters must be intriguing. Mystery books can be very expensive. Second, the way the crime was committed must be puzzling. Third, the discovery of the solution to the mystery must be very surprising.

Paragraph 6

Walking is an excellent family activity. Babies get fresh air. Children can become familiar with their neighborhood. Teenagers have an opportunity to talk to their parents. The sun feels warm in the summer. Parents get physical exercise and an opportunity to enjoy their kids.

Check your work on page 214.

PUTTING YOUR SKILLS TO WORK

Directions: Now you have a chance to practice writing a paragraph with a clear topic sentence and good supporting sentences. Take out your writing folder or notebook. Choose *one* of the following topics for your paragraph. Begin by writing a topic sentence. Then write at least four supporting sentences that relate to your topic sentence. Remember to write carefully and correctly, using the skills you have learned in this book.

1. Write a paragraph about your best qualities. What are the good things about you?

2. Think of something that is important to you. Write a paragraph explaining why it is so important.

☑ *Writing Checklist*

❑ Does your paragraph have a clear topic sentence?

❑ Do all your supporting sentences relate to the topic sentence?

❑ Do all your verbs show the right tense?

YOUR TURN TO WRITE
THREE PARAGRAPHS

This is it. You now have a chance to put to work all your writing skills. You will be writing three paragraphs. The first paragraph will describe a place or a person. The second will tell a story, and the third will state an opinion.

Make sure each paragraph has a good topic sentence. Write carefully and correctly, using the skills you have learned in this book.

WRITING ASSIGNMENT

Part 1: Descriptive Paragraph

Directions: In this paragraph, you will describe a place or person. Use many adjectives to create an interesting word picture. If you choose a place, you might describe what you see as you look from left to right. Be certain to include any sounds or smells. If you choose a person, you might tell what he or she looks like—clothes, walk, speech.

Part 2: Story Paragraph

Directions: In this paragraph, tell a story about a very happy or sad event. First, tell what happened that led up to the event. Second, tell what happened during the event. Finally, tell what happened after the event. Remembering these three steps will always help you organize a story.

Part 3: Opinion Paragraph

Directions: For this final paragraph, you will write an opinion. You can begin by using one of these two topic sentences:

Writing is a very useful skill.
Writing is not a very useful skill.

You may also choose another opinion to write about. When writing this paragraph, make certain that the supporting sentences tell only why your opinion is a good one. You want to be as convincing as possible.

☑ Writing Checklist

❑ Does each paragraph have a topic sentence?

❑ Have you used colorful adjectives in the first paragraph?

❑ Is there a "before, during, and after" in the second paragraph?

❑ Did you support your opinion clearly in the final paragraph?

LANGUAGE SKILLS
A COMPLETE REVIEW

The time has come to see how much you can remember from the information in this book. The following material will give you an opportunity to review almost every area you have studied.

PARTS OF SPEECH

Part of Speech	Definition
Noun	Names a person, place, thing or idea
Pronoun	Takes the place of a noun
Verb	An action or linking word
Adjective	Describes a noun and tells what kind, which one, or how many
Adverb	Describes a verb and tells how, when, or where

EXERCISE 7: PARTS OF SPEECH

Directions: Read the sentences that follow. One word is underlined in each sentence. Decide what part of speech each underlined word is (noun, pronoun, verb, adjective, or adverb). The first one is done as an example.

1. A landlord <u>demands</u> the rent on time.   *verb*

2. <u>He</u> is responsible for apartment maintenance.   _____

3. At times, getting repairs done <u>is</u> almost impossible.   _____

4. Tenants must ask <u>repeatedly</u> for assistance.   _____

5. <u>Assertive</u> tenants get the best service.   _____

6. Some <u>rents</u> are too high for the size of the apartment.   _____

7. In cities, people pay <u>dearly</u> for a rental property.   _____

8. A $425 city apartment <u>costs</u> $325 in a small town.   _____

9. Some <u>exclusive</u> apartments refuse pets and children.   _____

10. <u>Adults</u> often prefer quiet living areas.   _____

Check your work on page 214.

EXERCISE 8: TYPES OF SENTENCES

Directions: In this exercise, you will read groups of three sentences. Place the correct punctuation at the end of each sentence. In the blank following each sentence, tell whether it is a statement, a question, a command, or an exclamation. The first one in the first group is done as an example.

1. a. There are days when I am very tired.   *statement*
   b. Why am I so tired on some days   _____
   c. I am sick of being so darn tired   _____

2. a. Chan is planning to give a party   _____
   b. Is Chan planning to give a party   _____
   c. Give a party, Chan   _____

3. a. Working the night shift is very stressful   _____
   b. Is working the night shift very stressful   _____
   c. I can't stand the night shift anymore   _____

Check your work on page 215.

FINDING THE SUBJECT AND VERB

The subject of a sentence is the person, place, thing, or idea talked about in the sentence. The verb tells what the subject is or does. In this sentence, the subject is *Bats* and the verb is *live*.

Bats live in the barn.

The next example is a command. In a command, the subject is always the missing *you*. The verb in this command is *Leave*.

Leave the bats alone. (*You* leave the bats alone.)

In a question, part of the verb often comes before the subject. In the following question, the subject is *Mickey* and the verb is *Did see*.

Did Mickey see the bats? (*Mickey did see the bats.*)

Sometimes words and phrases come between the subject and the verb. In the following sentence, the subject is *bats* and the verb is *hang*.

The bats in the barn hang from the rafters.

EXERCISE 9: FINDING THE SUBJECT AND THE VERB

Directions: Write the subject of each of the following sentences in the blank. Underline the verb. (Some of the verbs have two parts.) The first one is done as an example.

1. <u>Will</u> Jan <u>answer</u> the telephone? _____*Jan*_____

2. The shirts with short sleeves are on sale. _____

3. Daffodils bloom in April. _____

4. Make some coffee, please. _____

5. Does the blender work? _____

6. In that survey, people gave their opinions. _____

Check your work on page 215.

ADDING ADJECTIVES AND ADVERBS

Sentences need only a subject and a verb to make sense. Here are a few simple sentences:

Sam works.
A tree fell.
The car crashed.

Those sentences all tell complete thoughts. However, they are not very colorful or interesting because there are no descriptive words in them. In the following exercise, you will be adding color to sentences by adding adjectives and adverbs, like this:

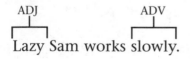

Lazy Sam works slowly.

EXERCISE 10: ADDING ADJECTIVES AND ADVERBS

Directions: Put an adjective in the blank in front of the noun in each of these sentences. Put an adverb in the blank after each verb. The first one is done as an example.

1. _____*Lazy*_____ Sam works _____*slowly*_____.

2. The _____ car crashed _____.

3. A _____ tree fell _____.

4. _____ motorcycles roar _____.

5. His _____ jacket tore _____.

Check your work on page 215.

EXERCISE 11: ACCURATE ADJECTIVES AND ADVERBS

Directions: Underline either the adjective or the adverb to complete each of the following sentences.

1. Jasper dashes *(wild, wildly)* through the house.

2. *(Mild, Mildly)* soap is better for your skin.

3. His *(heavy, heavily)* footsteps were heard on the front porch.

4. Move *(quick, quickly)*, or you'll be left behind.

5. The *(noisy, noisily)* motorcycle roared past the open window.

Check your work on page 215.

EXERCISE 12: CORRECT FORMS OF NOUNS AND PRONOUNS

Directions: Each of the following sentences contains one error related to using nouns and pronouns. Cross out the error in each sentence and write in the correction. The first one is done as an example.

1. Country ~~Life~~ *life* is a lot of work.

2. Farmer's must tend their fields daily.

3. Women on farms spend much of her time preserving food.

4. Childs help with the chores.

5. Its hard for a farmer to take a vacation.

6. Farmers hope their Harvests will make the work worthwhile.

Check your work on page 215.

EXERCISE 13: WRITING VERBS CORRECTLY

Directions: Write the correct form of the base verb in the blank. Use the tense you are given at the beginning of each sentence. Don't forget subject-verb agreement! The first one is done as an example.

1. *(present)* I _____*walk*_____ to work every day.
            (walk)

2. *(past)* Mr. Delmonico _____ for joy.
                        (jump)

3. *(present)* Time _____ more valuable as we grow older.
                    (become)

4. *(future)* Roger _____ Patrice the contract tomorrow.
                    (bring)

5. *(present)* The boy with the toy cars _____ the flu.
                                (have)

6. *(present)* They _____ waiting for you at the pool.
                    (be)

Check your work on page 215.

SUBJECT-VERB AGREEMENT WITH COMPOUND SUBJECTS

Remember these rules when making compound subjects agree with verbs:

1. Subjects joined by *and* always take the plural form of a verb.

    Ron and Nanette cook fantastically.

2. When subjects are joined by *or* or *nor*, the verb agrees with the part of the subject closest to it.

    Neither Ron nor Nanette **cooks** fantastically.
    Either their daughter or their sons **cook** fantastically.

EXERCISE 14: SUBJECT-VERB AGREEMENT WITH COMPOUND SUBJECTS

Directions: Read the following sentences. If the verb in a sentence does not agree with the subject, cross out the verb and write the correct form above it. If the sentence is correct, leave it as is.

1. The police and the firefighters were planning a fundraiser.

2. At closing time, the employees or the manager have to set the alarms.

3. Death and taxes is inevitable.

4. Knowledge or wisdom are a great gift.

5. Neither Charlie nor Tanya has the tickets.

6. The politicians and the mayor is planning a new city government.

7. The Salvation Army or the local charities are supporting a clothing bank.

Check your work on page 215.

THREE WAYS TO COMBINE SENTENCES

You learned the following three ways to combine whole sentences:

1. Use a comma with a conjunction (*and, but, yet, so, for, or, nor*).

    Phillip did a great job, **so** his boss gave him a bonus.

2. Use a semicolon, a connector, and a comma. You worked with these connectors: *consequently, furthermore, however, instead, moreover, nevertheless, therefore.*

    Phillip did a great job; **therefore**, his boss gave him a bonus.

3. Use a subordinating conjunction such as *because, since, though, although, if, when, after,* or *before*. When the subordinating conjunction is the first word in the combined sentence, put a comma between the two ideas.

    Because Phillip did a great job, his boss gave him a bonus.
    Phillip's boss gave him a bonus **because** he did a great job.

EXERCISE 15: USING CONJUNCTIONS CORRECTLY

Directions: You are given two choices for combining each of the following pairs of sentences. Circle the letter of the choice that combines each pair correctly. Be sure that the meaning of the conjunction makes sense in the sentence you choose.

1. Arnold ran for the bus. He missed it.

    a. Arnold ran for the bus; therefore, he missed it.
    b. Arnold ran for the bus, but he missed it.

2. The car hit the telephone pole. The pole split in half.

    a. When the car hit the telephone pole, the pole split in half.
    b. When the car hit the telephone pole the pole split in half.

3. Floyd won the pie-eating contest. He is not hungry.

    a. Floyd won the pie-eating contest, for he is not hungry.
    b. Floyd won the pie-eating contest, so he is not hungry.

4. Pedro speaks Spanish and English. He is bilingual.

    a. Because Pedro speaks Spanish and English, he is bilingual.
    b. Pedro speaks Spanish and English, nor is he bilingual.

5. Was Betsey on the phone? Was Rob on the phone?

    a. Was Betsey on the phone, or was Rob on the phone?
    b. Was Betsey on the phone; therefore, was Rob on the phone?

6. The subway platform was packed. The trains were late.

    a. The subway platform was packed since the trains were late.
    b. The subway platform was packed since, the trains were late.

7. I answered the phone. No one was on the line.

    a. I answered the phone but no one was on the line.
    b. When I answered the phone, no one was on the line.

8. The cardinal built a nest in the evergreen. He stayed there all year.

    a. The cardinal built a nest in the evergreen; however, he stayed there all year.
    b. The cardinal built a nest in the evergreen; furthermore, he stayed there all year.

9. Elizabeth has five kids. She wants seven more.

    a. Elizabeth has five kids; however, she wants seven more.
    b. Elizabeth has five kids, she wants seven more.

10. The wrestlers were late. The crowd was angry.

   a. Before the wrestlers were late, the crowd was angry.

   b. The wrestlers were late; therefore, the crowd was angry.

Check your work on page 215.

PUNCTUATING PERFECTLY

Punctuation Mark	Purpose
Period (.)	• Ends a statement • Ends most commands
Question mark (?)	• Ends a question
Exclamation point (!)	• Ends an exclamation
Comma (,)	• Separates items in a series of more than two items • Sets off interrupters • Sets off the name of the person being addressed • Used to combine sentences
Semicolon (;)	• Used to combine sentences
Colon (:)	• Used in greeting of a business letter
Quotation marks (" ")	• Set off a direct quotation
Apostrophe (')	• Shows possession • Replaces missing letter in a contraction

EXERCISE 16: PRACTICING PUNCTUATION

Directions: Each of the sentences in this exercise is missing one or two punctuation marks. Punctuate each sentence correctly. The first one is done as an example.

1. Do you think women make good politicians *?*

2. Just say no, say actors in TV commercials about drugs.

3. Open this door right this minute

4. Rose Allan a teacher, will retire soon.

5. Please order catfish, hush puppies and black coffee.

6. Cant you ever be on time for work?

7. All of the employees in fact must answer this questionnaire.

Check your work on page 215.

THE MECHANICS OF LETTER WRITING

Personal Letter	Business Letter
• Date in upper right corner • Comma between day and year • Greeting followed by comma • Body (Information) • Closing followed by comma • Signature	• Return address and date in upper right-hand corner • Comma between city and state and between day and year • Inside address on left above greeting—comma between city and state • Greeting followed by colon • Body (Information) • Closing followed by comma • Signature

EXERCISE 17: WRITING A PERSONAL LETTER

Directions: On a separate sheet of paper, write a personal letter of at least five sentences to someone you know. Tell the person anything you like. Use correct form and punctuation.

Check your work on page 216.

EXERCISE 18: DESCRIBING PHRASES AND PARALLEL STRUCTURE

Directions: Each of the following sentences contains either a misplaced describing phrase or incorrect parallel structure. Rewrite each sentence so it is written correctly and clearly.

1. The cat meowed, whined, and was scratching the door.

   _____

2. Getting a new job and to move to another apartment will improve Flo's life.

   _____

3. The children listened to the story of *The Pokey Little Puppy* eating their cookies.

   _____

4. Grabbing the ball and fighting to the goal line, we watched the quarterback.

_____

5. The family worked, played, and was living in Missouri for six years.

_____

6. Everyone should stop, look, and listening before crossing a street.

_____

7. Joe paid $500 for the used car of his hard-earned money.

_____

Check your answers on page 216.

POST-TEST

The post-test will give you a chance to see how much you remember about the information you studied in this book. Take the test without looking back for help or answers.

The post-test has been divided into two sections. The first section is a test of your overall knowledge of language skills. The second section is a test of your writing ability and asks you to write a paragraph.

Once you complete the test, check your answers with those starting on page 197. Then fill out the evaluation chart. This chart will tell you which sections of the book you might want to review.

SECTION I

PART 1: NOUNS AND PRONOUNS

This section tests your knowledge of nouns: common and proper nouns, singular and plural nouns, and possessive nouns. It also tests your knowledge of pronouns: subject, object, and possessive.

Directions: Each of the following sentences has an underlined part. Below each sentence are three options for writing the underlined part. Choose the option that makes the sentence correct. The first option is always the same as the underlined part of the original sentence.

1. <u>Both Tom and Jeff wanted to be elected Captain</u> of the community softball team.

   (1) Both Tom and Jeff wanted to be elected Captain
   (2) Both Tom and Jeff wanted to be elected captain
   (3) both Tom and Jeff wanted to be elected captain

2. <u>They</u> have played on the team for five years.

   (1) They
   (2) Them
   (3) Their

3. <u>Their</u> both excellent softball players.

   (1) Their
   (2) Theirs
   (3) They're

4. On Saturday, the <u>players</u> votes were counted.

   (1) players
   (2) players'
   (3) player's

5. The <u>men</u> with the most votes was Jeff.

   (1) men
   (2) mans
   (3) man

6. <u>His</u> job will be to lead the players for one season.

   (1) His
   (2) He's
   (3) He

7. Jeff will assign <u>they</u> to their positions.

   (1) they
   (2) them
   (3) him

8. During practice, he will watch all the <u>pitchs</u> closely.

   (1) pitchs
   (2) pitch's
   (3) pitches

9. The games will be played at <u>Hope Valley park</u>.

   (1) Hope Valley park
   (2) Hope valley park
   (3) Hope Valley Park

10. Jeff will plan the <u>teams</u> strategy for each game.

   (1) teams
   (2) team's
   (3) team'

PART 2: VERBS

This section tests your knowledge of verbs: forming verb tenses, using time clues to verb tense, irregular verb forms, and subject-verb agreement.

Directions: Underline the correct form of the verb to complete each sentence.

1. The students in the class *(are, is)* happy with their grades.

2. Your advice *(were, was)* what saved our garden.

3. Next week, Jim *(will race, raced)* in the track meet.

4. The manager *(plan, plans)* to quit her job after payday.

5. The strength of these workers *(make, makes)* any job easy.

6. Last night, Sheila *(announces, announced)* her engagement.

7. Bill or I *(drive, drives)* the car pool every Wednesday.

8. Right now Uncle Ray *(is standing, was standing)* on his head.

9. You *(have, has)* got to tell Bruce the truth.

10. My uncles *(tell, tells)* terrible jokes.

11. They *(do, does)* their taxes on April 15th every year.

12. You *(turn, turns)* left at the second traffic light.

13. Someday Laura *(will learn, learns)* to stay out of trouble.

14. It *(give, gives)* me the creeps.

15. Tiffany and Sandy *(spend, spends)* a lot of time in the bathroom.

PART 3: SENTENCE STRUCTURE

This section tests your knowledge of different methods for combining ideas in sentences: using joining words, describing phrases, and parallel structure.

Directions: Each of the following sentences has an underlined part. Below each sentence are three options for writing the underlined part. Choose the option that makes the sentence correct. The first option is always the same as the underlined part of the original sentence.

1. The rain lasted for three <u>days, but</u> the rivers were flooded.

    (1) days, but
    (2) days; so
    (3) days, so

2. The fish <u>are frying in the pan that we caught at the lake</u>.

    (1) are frying in the pan that we caught at the lake
    (2) that we caught at the lake are frying in the pan
    (3) are frying in the lake that we caught in the pan

3. The nurse smelled <u>smoke, however, she</u> called for help.

    (1) smoke, however, she
    (2) smoke; however, she
    (3) smoke; consequently, she

4. The president talked, laughed, and <u>he was joking</u>.

    (1) he was joking
    (2) he joked
    (3) joked

5. <u>Sally bumped into the table walking across the room.</u>

   (1) Sally bumped into the table walking across the room.
   (2) Walking across the room, Sally bumped into the table.
   (3) Walking across the room, the table bumped into Sally.

6. When the curtain <u>fell the</u> audience cheered.

   (1) fell the
   (2) fell; the
   (3) fell, the

7. I made the <u>coffee and</u> I drank it all.

   (1) coffee and
   (2) coffee or
   (3) coffee, and

8. Farhad wants his family to come to the United <u>States; therefore, he</u> is saving money for their tickets.

   (1) States; therefore, he
   (2) States; instead, he
   (3) States; nevertheless, he

9. Jennifer can take the <u>job if, she</u> buys a car.

   (1) job if, she
   (2) job, if she
   (3) job if she

10. Norma is <u>tired, but</u> she is still working.

   (1) tired, but
   (2) tired, so
   (3) tired, before

PART 4: PUNCTUATION

This section tests your knowledge of many punctuation marks you have studied in this text.

Directions: Only one of the sentences in each of the following groups is punctuated correctly. Circle the number of the correct sentence.

1. (1) Terry screamed, "Shut the door."
   (2) Terry screamed, "Shut the door!"
   (3) Terry screamed, Shut the door!

2. (1) Sandy, will you please give me a call?
   (2) Sandy will you please give me a call?
   (3) Sandy, will you please give me a call.

3. (1) Mrs. Popovich a true friend, cooked dinner for me.
   (2) Mrs. Popovich a true friend cooked dinner for me.
   (3) Mrs. Popovich, a true friend, cooked dinner for me.

4. (1) The movers can't get the piano up the stairs.
   (2) The movers cant' get the piano up the stairs.
   (3) The movers cant get the piano up the stairs.

5. (1) For example the cake could be green and white.
   (2) For example, the cake could be green and white.
   (3) For example, the cake could be green, and white.

6. (1) Science, English math, and literature are important subjects
       to study.
   (2) Science English math and literature are important subjects
       to study.
   (3) Science, English, math, and literature are important subjects
       to study.

SECTION II
WRITING A PARAGRAPH

Directions: This section of the test will give you a chance to demonstrate how well you write. Pick just one of the three suggested topics. Read the choices carefully. You should brainstorm or cluster ideas before you begin writing. When you finish writing, go back and reread what you have written. Check to be certain that you have used the information you learned about writing paragraphs. Also check spelling, capitalization, punctuation, and sentence structure. Then make any needed changes.

TOPIC 1

Think of a person that you admire—a close friend, a coworker, a parent, or any person you think highly of. In a paragraph, explain why you admire that person. What things about the person do you respect most?

TOPIC 2

Imagine what your perfect job would be like. Where would you work? What would you do? Describe your perfect job in a paragraph with lots of details.

TOPIC 3

Almost all of us have a good love story to tell, whether it is about ourselves or someone else. Think of a love story you could tell. It could be sweet or sad, silly or serious, or some of each. Write a paragraph telling your love story.

Check your work on pages 197–198.

POST-TEST ANSWER KEY
Section I
Part 1: Nouns and Pronouns

1. (2) The noun *captain* should not be capitalized because it is not used as a person's title.
2. (1) No correction is necessary.
3. (3) If you substitute *They are* in the sentence, it makes sense.
4. (2) The plural noun must be made possessive.
5. (3) Only one man could have gotten the most votes.
6. (1) No correction is necessary.
7. (2) The object pronoun must be used because it is not the subject of the sentence. The pronoun must be plural to agree with *their*.
8. (3) When a noun ends in *ch*, add *es* to make it plural.
9. (3) All three words should be capitalized to show that this is the specific name of the park.
10. (2) The noun must be made possessive.

Part 2: Verbs

1. are — The verb must agree with the plural subject *students*.
2. was — The subject, *advice*, is singular.
3. will race — The time clue *Next week* tells you to use the future tense.
4. plans — The subject, *manager*, is singular.
5. makes — The subject is *strength*, a singular noun.
6. announced — The time clue *Last night* tells you to use the past tense.
7. drive — The two parts of the subject are joined by *or*. The verb must agree with the closest part of the subject, *I*.
8. is standing — The time clue *Right now* tells you to use the present continuing tense.
9. have — Use *have* to agree with *You*.
10. tell — The subject, *uncles*, is plural.
11. do — This verb form agrees with *They*.
12. turn — This verb form agrees with *You*.
13. will — The time clue *Some learn day* tells you to use the future tense.
14. gives — This verb form agrees with *It*.
15. spend — The parts of the subject are joined by *and*, so the subject is plural.

Part 3: Sentence Structure

1. (3) The conjunction *so* shows that the first part of the sentence caused the second part.
2. (2) The original sentence says that we caught the pan at the lake. The describing phrase *that we caught at the lake* should be placed next to *fish*.
3. (3) The connector *consequently* shows that the first part of the sentence caused the second part. Note also the correct punctuation for this connector.
4. (3) For parallel structure, the items *talked*, *laughed*, and *joked* must be in the same form.
5. (2) The original sentence says that the table was walking across the room. The describing phrase *walking across the room* must be placed next to *Sally*.
6. (3) When a subordinating conjunction comes first in a sentence, the two ideas in the sentence are separated by a comma.
7. (3) This sentence contains two complete thoughts, so they must be separated by a comma.
8. (1) No correction is necessary.
9. (3) No comma is needed when the subordinating conjunction comes in the middle of the sentence.
10. (1) No correction is necessary.

Part 4: Punctuation

1. (2) This sentence contains a direct quote that shows strong emotion.
2. (1) This sentence is a question. The name *Sandy* is used in direct address and must be set off with a comma.
3. (3) The renaming phrase *a true friend* must be set off by commas.

4. (1) The apostrophe takes the place of the missing letters when the word *cannot* is made into a contraction.

5. (2) The interrupting phrase *For example* must be set off with a comma. No comma should be used after *green* because *and* is not used to join two complete thoughts.

6. (3) Commas must be placed after every item in a series except the last one.

Section II
Writing a Paragraph

In this section of the post-test, you had to write a paragraph on your own. If possible, have an instructor work with you to evaluate your paragraph. If you are evaluating your paragraph on your own, be sure to put it aside for a day or two first. Then use the following questions to help you.

1. Does your paragraph have a clear topic sentence? Topic sentences are explained on pages 176-78.

2. Do the other sentences in the paragraph support the topic sentence? Supporting sentences are discussed on pages 176-78.

3. Did you have trouble coming up with ideas to put in your paragraph? If so, review clustering on pages 24-25 and brainstorming on pages 96-97.

4. Did you have trouble with verbs, pronouns, commas, or other areas of grammar? If so, you can find pages to review in the Table of Contents.

If you want to try writing another paragraph, go back to Section II of the post-test on page 196. Choose another of the topics to write about and evaluate it in the same way. Remember, the best way to improve your writing is to write!

POST-TEST EVALUATION CHART

Check your answers on pages 197–198. Then find the number of each question you missed on the chart and circle it in the second column. Then you will know which pages you might need to review. You may also want to work your way through "A Complete Review," pages 180–189.

	Item Number	Review Pages	Number Correct
Part 1: Nouns and Pronouns			
Nouns	1, 4, 5, 8, 9, 10	45–55	
Pronouns	3, 7, 2, 6	55–65	_____ /10
Part 2: Verbs			
Verb tense	3, 6, 8, 13	70–88	
Subject-verb agreement	1, 2, 4, 5, 7, 9, 10, 11, 12, 14, 15	98–110	_____ /15
Part 3: Sentence Structure			
Conjunctions	1, 7, 10	146–150	
Connectors	3, 8	151–155	
Describing phrases	2, 5	167–171	
Parallel structure	4	171–174	
Subordinating conjunctons	6, 9	156–159	_____ /10
Part 4: Punctuation			
Quotation marks	1	88–90	
Types of sentences	2	29–31	
Contractions	4	62–65	
Commas	3, 5, 6	110–115 131–134	_____ /6

ANSWER KEY

CHAPTER 1

Exercise 1: Identifying Nouns
page 13
1. Dan, motorcycle, speed
2. Mr. Archer, stadium, baseball
3. Knoxville, Shelley, fashion
4. Aunt Rose, shells, ocean
5. lawyer, bail, courthouse
6. president, dog, White House

Exercise 2: Writing Nouns
page 13
Your answers will be different from these. Compare your answers to these sample answers to see if you used similar nouns.
1. Mark
2. mother
3. Alaska
4. couch
5. diamond
6. Courage

Exercise 3: Identifying Pronouns
page 15
1. He, it
2. He, he
3. she, it
4. She, them, us
5. He, me
6. He, his

Exercise 4: Writing Pronouns
page 15
1. It
2. He
3. They
4. It
5. He or She
6. it

Exercise 5: Identifying Verbs
page 17
1. rides
2. goes, is
3. found, visited
4. finds
5. are
6. kept

Exercise 6: Writing Verbs
page 17
Your answers will differ from these. Did you fill in all the blanks with the right kinds of action verbs?
1. hop, jump, walk, run, skip
2. sew, draw, paint, write, build
3. breathe, see, talk, hear, smell
4. dream, think, decide, fantasize, invent
5. sleep, swim, float, exercise, relax

Exercise 7: Identifying Adjectives
pages 18–19
1. Daring, red, high
2. wonderful, exciting
3. new, fuzzy
4. big, little, beautiful
5. kind, old,
6. noisy, busy

Exercise 8: Writing Adjectives
page 19
Your answers will be different from these. Make sure that you used adjectives in your answers.

	You	Your home	Your father
1.	smart	new	tough
2.	handsome	tiny	old
3.	likable	two-story	tan
4.	jealous	vinyl-sided	wrinkled
5.	sad	expensive	cheerful

Exercise 9: Identifying Adverbs
page 21
1. dangerously
2. early
3. there
4. carefully
5. immediately
6. loudly

Exercise 10: Writing Adverbs
page 21
You may have thought of different adverbs from the ones listed here. Make sure the adverbs you chose tell how, when, and where depending on the instructions.
1. sweetly, wildly, or quickly
2. daily, now, or constantly
3. upstairs, there, or outdoors
4. sweetly, wildly, or quickly
5. daily, now, or constantly
6. upstairs, there, or outdoors

Exercise 11: Chapter Review
page 22
Part 1

Nouns	Pronouns	Verbs
Mr. Archer	he	listens
dog	they	keep
baseball	you	went
motorcycle	it	find
boat	me	loves

Adjectives	Adverbs
neat	early
red	there
happy	slowly
old	angrily
nice	now

Part 2

Check to see if you added the correct part of speech to the sentences. You might have a different word, but the part of speech will be the same.

1. motorcycle   noun
2. goes   verb
3. fuzzy   adjective
4. carefully   adverb
5. its   pronoun

CHAPTER 2

Exercise 1: Identifying Sentences and Fragments
pages 27–28

1. S	4. S	7. S	10. S
2. F	5. F	8. S	
3. F	6. S	9. F	

Exercise 2: Turning Fragments into Sentences
page 28

You won't have written the same sentences as these. Just make sure that each of your sentences tells a complete thought.

1. The police took the man to jail.
2. The man was very angry.
3. An officer locked him up.
4. He called his lawyer.
5. The man stayed in jail overnight.
6. He did not want to sleep in jail.
7. He felt terrible.

Exercise 3: Types of Sentences
page 31

1. This is the Rainbow Coffee Shop.
   statement
2. Would you like to see a menu?
   question
3. Get me a glass of water.
   command
4. The food here is supposed to be awful.
   statement
5. Do you smell smoke coming from the kitchen?
   question
6. This place is on fire!
   exclamation

Exercise 4: Mistakes in Sentences
page 32

1. The rents here are sky-high.
   (The original group of words was a fragment. The answer must be a complete sentence.)
2. It is difficult to find a new apartment.
3. Why did they have to tear our building down?
4. Only three months till we have to move.
   (The original group of words was a fragment. Your answer must be a complete sentence.)
5. Most landlords won't permit pets.
6. I can't give up my dog!
   (The original group of words was a fragment. Your answer must be a complete sentence.)

Exercise 5: Finding the Subject
page 34

	Subject	Verb
1.	Chicago	is
2.	People	live
3.	Trains	take
4.	The buildings	are
5.	The wind	blows
6.	People	hurry
7.	Workers	ride

Exercise 6: Finding Tricky Subjects
pages 35–36

1. Denise
2. Sarah
3. *(You)*
4. Larry
5. the coffee
6. *(You)*
7. we
8. The workers
9. *(You)*
10. you

Exercise 7: Writing Subjects
page 36

Only you can be sure if your answers are correct. Look over your answers. Have you answered using the names of persons, places, and things you are familiar with?

Exercise 8: Writing Action Predicates
page 37
Make sure that the predicate you wrote is an action verb.

1. Babies cry.
2. Smoke rises.
3. Parrots talk.
4. Flowers grow.
5. Cats meow.
6. Dogs bark.
7. Birds chirp.
8. Fish swim.
9. Mosquitoes bite.
10. Scissors cut.

Exercise 9: Writing Linking Predicates
page 37
Make sure that you used a linking verb in each of your predicates.

1. Mary is happy.
2. The tomatoes are red.
3. The pool is open.
4. My apartment is neat.
5. Bicycles are fun.
6. The dog is ugly.
7. Dad is busy.
8. His motorcycle was stolen.
9. Our money is gone.
10. Summer is hot.

Exercise 10: Chapter Review
pages 40–42
Part 1

1. Every sentence has **two** parts. They are the **subject** and the **predicate**. In sentences, the **subject** is a person, place, thing, or idea, and verbs are used in the **predicates**.
2. There are four types of sentences. A sentence that simply says something is a **statement**. A sentence that demands that something be done is a **command**. A sentence that asks something is a **question**. And a sentence that shows very strong emotion is an **exclamation**.

Part 2
1. Juan
2. A counselor
3. Juan
4. This company
5. The interviewer
6. You (In a command, the subject is always the missing *you*.)
7. Rona

Part 3
1. d
2. a
3. c
4. b
5. e

Part 4
Here are some sample answers. Your answers will be different.

1. A person is cooking in this picture. She might say, "I am making breakfast." *(statement)*
2. A person is in a store being waited on in this picture. The clerk might be saying, "May I help you?" *(question)*
3. A person is about to be hit by a car in this picture. She might shout, "You're going to hit me!" *(exclamation)*
4. A dog is being sent outside in this picture. The man might be saying, "Go outside." *(command)*

CHAPTER 3

Exercise 1: Identifying Nouns
page 46

Nan loves her **dog**, **Fifi**. **Fifi** is a **poodle**. At the **beach**, **Nan** wants to be certain that **Fifi** does not get too hot. **Nan** bought a **stroller** with an **awning** so **Fifi** could be in the **shade** while on the **beach**. **Nan** also often buys **ice cream** for **Fifi**. Many **people** on the **beach** stare at the **poodle**. The **people** also stare at **Nan**!

Exercise 2: Common and Proper Nouns
page 47
Below are some sample answers. Did you capitalize your proper nouns?

1. Honda
2. Tommy
3. Lake Michigan
4. Senator Jesse Helms
5. Sears
6. Main Street
7. Aliquippa
8. Reverend Zeiders
9. Christmas
10. Vermont

11. China
12. Boy Scouts
13. Cook County
14. Dr. Owens

Exercise 3: Capitalizing Proper Nouns
page 49

1. Mrs. Linkowski first saw the **Washington Monument** when she was five.
2. If Tim has those symptoms again, call **Doctor Lee**.
3. **New Year's Eve** is **Aunt** Betty's favorite holiday.
4. My car is a **Ford Escort**.
5. Sam's favorite rock groups are the **Rolling Stones** and the **Grateful Dead**.
6. The teachers at **Brookmont Elementary School** wrote a letter to **Mayor Carlson**.
7. My dentist hasn't missed a **Green Bay Packers** game in seven years.
8. C
9. Ms. Davis is a member of an organization called **Mothers Against Drunk Driving**.
10. The **Oak Valley Fire Department** was too late to save the warehouse.

Exercise 4: Changing Singular Nouns to Plural
pages 51–52

1. Many **women** do not want to work outside the home.
2. They feel that all **children** should be reared by their mothers.
3. A lot of **books** say it is not right for women to work.
4. Some **women** argue that they must work to earn money.
5. Some **employers** pay women less than men.
6. **Salaries** should be the same for all people who do the same job.
7. Some companies have child care **programs**.
8. Often, several **churches** in a town have day care centers.
9. Many school **buses** will pick students up at the centers.
10. **Cities**, counties, and towns should do even more to help mothers who must work.

Exercise 5: Correcting Errors with Nouns
page 52

1. b
2. a
3. c
4. a
5. a

Exercise 6: Writing Possessive Nouns
page 54

1. coach's
2. coaches'
3. army's
4. armies'
5. James's
6. woman's
7. women's
8. choir's
9. choirs'
10. Yim's

Exercise 7: More Practice with Possessive Nouns
pages 54–55

1. cat's cradle
2. telephone's ring
3. busboys' trays
4. player's helmet
5. principal's office
6. Mickey's house
7. teachers' meetings
8. coach's signals
9. neighbors' anniversary
10. mechanic's wrench

Exercise 8: Using Subject Pronouns
page 57

1. She
2. He
3. He
4. They
5. It

Exercise 9: Using Object Pronouns
page 58

1. it
2. her
3. him
4. them
5. us
6. her
7. it
8. him

Exercise 10: Using Possessive Pronouns
pages 59–60
1. their
2. his
3. its
4. her
5. theirs
6. hers
7. their
8. ours

Exercise 11: Using Pronouns
page 60
Karen enjoys **her** job at the Adult Learning Center. **She** is the staff support specialist. She helps Larry with **his** teaching. Carol teaches there too and is well liked by **her** students. The students look forward to coming to **their** classes.

The directors of the center are Vicki and George. **They** count on government grants to fund the center's programs. **Their** assistant, Bob, helps **them** get funding for the programs. **He** is a very important member of the staff. All the Adult Learning Center staff members are quick to state, "**We** believe in adult education!"

Exercise 12: Pronoun Agreement
pages 61–62
1. he
2. She
3. his
4. them
5. They
6. their
7. it
8. Our

Exercise 13: Forming Contractions
page 63
1. they've
2. doesn't
3. he's
4. I'm
5. we're
6. isn't
7. shouldn't
8. they'll (Notice that two letters are removed in this contraction.)
9. wouldn't
10. that's

Exercise 14: Contractions and Possessive Pronouns
pages 64–65
It's always a good idea to decorate **your** home. Even people who don't have much spare time can hang pictures on **their** walls and put up curtains. Of course, **it's** harder if **you're** working full-time. Gary, a friend of mine, did a nice job on **his** apartment. I hope that he and **his** friend Pete will help me out. **They're** really talented at decorating.

Exercise 15: Chapter Review
pages 65–67
Part 1
1. c
2. a
3. a
4. a
5. c
6. b
7. Years ago, I went to hear **Senator** Stevenson speak.
8. My **aunt** always said he was her favorite **senator**.
9. The year **Stevenson** ran for president, **Dad** bought a new **Ford**.
10. I
11. his
12. She
13. hers
14. us
15. they
16. my
17. ours

Part 2
1. After the party, Dean stayed out very late.
(The original group of words was a fragment. Any answer is correct as long as you wrote a complete sentence.)
2. **Everyone** went to a local restaurant for dinner.
3. Look out—it's a raid!
4. **Stay** in your seats.
5. The gangsters will be arrested.
(The original group of words was a fragment. Any answer is correct as long as you wrote a complete sentence.)
6. you
7. Music

8. you (In a command, the subject is always the missing *you*.)
9. That DJ
10. news
11. Ilena

CHAPTER 4
Exercise 1: Choosing Present-Tense Verbs
page 73
1. (Americans) enjoy
2. (They) like
3. (I) love
4. (I) find
5. (They) welcome
6. (a church) sponsors
7. (A school) gives
8. (I) learn
9. (My parents) live
10. (We) write

Exercise 2: Writing the Past and Future Tenses
page 75

Past	Future
1. looked	will look
2. moved	will move
3. lived	will live
4. earned	will earn
5. saved	will save
6. played	will play

Exercise 3: Past Tense of Irregular Verbs
pages 76–77

1. gave	11. said
2. told	12. made
3. ran	13. went
4. became	14. sat
5. saw	15. did
6. took	16. had
7. taught	17. sold
8. came	18. drank
9. read	19. wrote
10. brought	20. ate

Exercise 4: Choosing the Correct Past-Tense Form
page 78
1. saw
2. ran
3. was
4. did
5. came
6. went

Exercise 5: Forms of *Be*
pages 79–80

1. were	6. were
2. are	7. is
3. was	8. are
4. is	9. was
5. is	10. was

Exercise 6: Forms of *Have*
page 81
1. has
2. has
3. will have
4. had
5. had
6. have
7. will have

Exercise 7: Forms of *Do*
page 82
1. Do
2. do
3. did
4. did
5. does
6. will do
7. does
8. will do
9. did
10. will do

Exercise 8: Using Time Clues
page 83

Verb	Time Clues
1. want	Today
2. worked	Last year
3. wake	Now
4. will go	Tomorrow
5. buy	These days
6. will run	Next week
7. exercised	Last week

Exercise 9: The Present Continuing Tense
page 86

1. is studying
2. are working
3. is learning
4. are writing
5. is changing
6. is helping
7. is communicating
8. am enjoying

Exercise 10: The Past Continuing Tense
pages 87–88

1. was raining
2. was driving
3. were smiling
4. were going
5. was looking
6. was giving
7. were blowing
8. was thinking
9. was yawning
10. was ringing
11. was dreaming

Exercise 11: Using Quotation Marks
pages 89–90

1. "I think the best years of a person's life are his teen years," said Raymond.
2. His mother laughed and said, "That's because you are a teenager."
3. "Actually, you will have more fun once you are an adult," said his twenty-two-year-old brother, John.
4. "What will happen to me once I reach thirty?" John wondered.
5. "You'll be on your way to forty, and believe me, those are really the best years," said Mom.
6. Dad piped in, "Oh, I don't know, I think I'm even better-looking at fifty."
7. John asked, "How were the sixties, Grandma?"
8. "They were great," Grandma responded.
9. "However, the seventies are the best," she said, smiling.
10. "I can say whatever I want, do whatever I want, and go wherever I want—senior citizenship is sensational!" Grandma exclaimed.

Exercise 12: Chapter Review
pages 91–94

Part 1

1. Past	Present	Future
sang	jump	will find
looked	swim	will write
flew	fall	will examine
danced	claim	will paint
diagnosed	drive	will walk
saw	are	will want
had	talk	will say
was	hopes	
drew	is	

2. b
3. c
4. a
5. c
6. a
7. b
8. c
9. c
10. c
11. b

Part 2

1. Her **children's** room is a mess.
2. Some children keep their **rooms** very neat and clean.
3. I **can't** blame her children for being messy.
4. **They're** just like her.
5. **She** doesn't like to clean her room either. (The original sentence was a fragment. You should have added a subject to make the sentence complete.)
6. **They** will all clean their rooms today.
7. A fragment does not tell a complete thought.
8. subject, predicate
9. capital letter

CHAPTER 5

Exercise 1: Subject-Verb Agreement with Pronouns
page 99

1. owns
2. take
3. come
4. get
5. fusses
6. thanks

Exercise 2: Subject-Verb Agreement with Irregular Verbs
page 101

1. are
2. have
3. am
4. does
5. was
6. do
7. has
8. do
9. were
10. are

Exercise 3: Singular and Plural Subjects
pages 103–104

1. is — *Summer* can be replaced by *It.*
2. loves — *Teresa* can be replaced by *She.*
3. makes — *Silence* can be replaced by *It.*
4. move — *Families* can be replaced by *They.*
5. look — *The gardens* can be replaced by *They.*
6. bring — *Colorado's ski slopes* can be replaced by *They.*
7. guides — *Carl* can be replaced by *He.*
8. gives — *Strength* can be replaced by *It.*

Exercise 4: Subject-Verb Agreement with Compound Subjects
page 106

1. increase — The parts are *The local police* and *the state police.* A compound subject joined by *and* is always plural.
2. is — The parts are *Relatives* and *a friend.* The verb agrees with *a friend* because the parts are joined by *or* and *a friend* is the closest part.
3. come — The parts are *Henry* and *his sisters.* A compound subject joined by *and* is always plural.
4. need — The parts are *You* and *your parents.* A compound subject joined by *and* is always plural.
5. go — The parts are *Nan* and *I.* The verb agrees with *I* because the parts are joined by *nor,* and *I* is the closest part.
6. give — The parts are *A local club* and *businesses.* The verb agrees with *businesses* because the parts are joined by *or,* and *businesses* is the closest part.
7. have — The parts are *coffee* and *sweets.* The verb agrees with *sweets* because the parts are joined by *nor* and *sweets* is the closest part.
8. help — The parts are *newspapers* and *radio.* A compound subject joined by *and* is always plural.

Exercise 5: Subject-Verb Agreement with Describing Phrases
pages 108–109

	Subject	Verb	Describing Phrase
1.	tree	changes	with the red and gold leaves
2.	children	pick	under the tree
3.	teacher	watches	in the green slacks
4.	father	arrives	of one of the girls
5.	Truckers	take	with good sense
6.	truck	has	with bad brakes
7.	driver	goes	on a long trip
8.	Truck stops	are	on the freeway

Exercise 6: Subject-Verb Agreement Review
pages 109–110

1. help — The compound subject is *Nutritious meals and rest.*
2. are — The subject is *They.*

3. say   The subject is *Clerks*.
4. believes   The subject is *Sally*.
5. give   The subject is *A grandmother and grandfather*.
6. go   The subject is *those blankets*.
7. do   The subject is *You*.
8. looks   The closest part of the compound subject is *meat*.
9. earn   The plural subject is *Women*.
10. cheer   The closest part of the subject is *flowers*.

Exercise 7: Commas with Phrases That Give Additional Information
page 111

1. The Wizard of Oz, a favorite childhood character, granted wishes.
2. Checkers, a game for two, is challenging for children and adults.
3. I like to have a hamburger or two at Moody's, a local drive-in.
4. Horror films, a frightening form of entertainment, attract big audiences.
5. The undercover policeman on the case is Detective Blackwell, a member of the vice squad.
6. Linda Chavez, the Republican candidate, lost the election.

Exercise 8: Phrases That Connect or Make Transitions Between Ideas
pages 112–113

1. My best friend, of course, would never go out with my boyfriend.
2. On one hand, Bruce wants very much to have children.
3. On the other hand, he is worried about all the responsibility.
4. I just learned, in fact, that I'm eating all the wrong foods.
5. Marlene gave up smoking, by the way.
6. Andy, in my opinion, is not mature enough to live on his own.

Exercise 9: Commas In Direct Address
page 113

1. Terry, will you please come for a visit this summer?
2. If I could afford the trip, Mary, I would surely come.
3. Mr. Gregson, you are a very lucky man.
4. Do you realize how talented you are, Paula?
5. In two weeks, Mrs. Grant, your lease will expire.

Exercise 10: Review of Commas
page 114

1. Tim, my first cousin, is coming to live with us.
2. He arrives tomorrow, in fact.
3. Mrs. Brown, the lady across the street, said she might be able to get him a job.
4. We hope, Ms. Coleman, that you are prepared for the worst.
5. Will you work overtime, Beth?
6. Life in a big city is, of course, both exciting and scary.
7. Felix, a friend from my hometown, convinced me to go back to school.

Exercise 11: Chapter Review
pages 115–117
Part 1

1. Subject-verb agreement is making the verb in a sentence agree with the subject of that sentence.
2. end in *s*
3. end in *s*
4. A compound subject is in two parts.
5. Lucas and Dena **want** to buy a house.
6. They **are** looking on the east side of town.
7. A porch or patio **gives** a house an outdoor feeling.
8. Lucas, an excellent cook**,** examines the kitchens carefully.
9. Sunlight **is** important to Dena.
10. The house with the hardwood floors **was** too expensive.
11. Neither Lucas nor Dena **likes** the less expensive houses.
12. They are**,** in fact, afraid that they will never find a good house for what they can pay.

Part 2

1. A common noun is the general name of a person, place, thing, or idea. A proper noun is the specific

name of a person, place, thing,
or idea and is always capitalized.

2. A sentence tells a complete thought.
A fragment does not tell a
complete thought.

3. apostrophe + *s ('s)*

4. will

5. **Bob's** car looks brand-new.

6. He is very careful to maintain
it properly.

7. **The** required oil change is done
every 3,000 miles.

8. **He** rotates the tires every
7,500 miles.

9. Last month, he **changed** the gas filter,
the oil, and the spark plugs.

10. The best thing to do for a car
is to maintain it well. (The original
sentence is a fragment. Any answer
that is a complete sentence is correct.)

11. A well-kept car will **last** for years.

12. **Its** paint can be preserved with
regular waxing.

CHAPTER 6

Exercise 1: Choosing Adjectives
page 122

You will probably have chosen one of
the following adjectives to complete
each sentence.

1. Hectic or Busy

2. busy, colorful, many, or numerous

3. many, busy, numerous, or frustrated

4. Frustrated or Busy

5. small, inexpensive, expensive,
many, or numerous

6. Colorful, Many, or Numerous

7. expensive, many, gigantic, or
numerous

8. inexpensive or small

9. gigantic, expensive, or numerous

10. Numerous, Many, or Frustrated

Exercise 2: Using Adjectives
pages 122–123

Your answers should be similar to these.
These answers were written by
another student.

1. The **middle-aged** men play **forty**
games of poker once a month.

2. They use **playing** cards and play
on a **card** table.

3. The game is played on the **second** Friday
of each month.

4. The bets are **low.**

5. During the **monthly** game, **two** pounds
of potato chips are eaten.

Exercise 3: Identifying Adjectives
page 124

The adjectives you should have circled are
listed below.

1. educational

2. informative

3. Many

4. tired

5. Silly

6. absurd

7. stupid

8. These

9. popular

10. violent

Exercise 4: Choosing Adverbs
page 126

As in Exercise 1, many of these sentences
have more than one possible answer.

1. *Hysterically, strangely,* or *nervously* can
tell how he laughed.

2. *Before* tells when he smiled.

3. *Outside* tells where he grinned.

4. *Patiently* or *nervously* can tell how she
stood.

5. *Strangely, threateningly,* or *nervously* can
tell how people looked.

6. *Rapidly* tells how his tears flowed.

7. *Down* tells where he fell.

8. *Threateningly, nervously,* or *abruptly* can
tell how she said, "Get up."

9. *Nervously, strangely,* or *hysterically* can
tell how he giggled.

10. *Abruptly* or *hysterically* can tell how he
stated, "No one would understand."

Exercise 5: Writing Sentences with Adverbs
pages 126–127

Your answers will differ from these. Check to
be sure you have used an adverb to modify
the verb in each of your sentences.

1. *(how)*   The students write carefully.
   (when)   We write daily.
   (where)   George writes here.

2. *(how)*   Melinda and Todd
                dance beautifully.
  (when)   She will dance tomorrow.
  (where)   Tim and Lena dance outside.
3. *(how)*   I read rapidly.
  (when)   Tom read the book yesterday.
  (where)   Sam will read here.

Exercise 6: Identifying Adverbs
page 128
Listed below are the adverbs you
should have circled.
  1. far
  2. early
  3. dangerously
  4. carefully
  5. Mysteriously
  6. angrily
  7. calmly
  8. everywhere
  9. there
  10. always

Exercise 7: Choosing Adjectives
or Adverbs
pages 130–131
  1. *Fantastic* is an adjective describing
     what kind of football season.
  2. *Carefully* is an adverb describing
     how a fan gets ready.
  3. *Calmly* is an adverb describing
     how he waits.
  4. *Excited* is an adjective describing
     what kind of crowd.
  5. *Loudly* is an adverb describing
     how the fan applauds.
  6. *Angrily* is an adverb describing *how*
     the crowd turns.
  7. *Suddenly* is an adverb describing
     when he realizes he is in enemy
     territory.
  8. *Cheerful* is an adjective describing
     what kind of smile.
  9. *Interesting* is an adjective describing
     what kind of game.
  10. *Magnificent* is an adjective
     describing *what kind* of pass.

Exercise 8: Using Commas in
a Series
page 133
The necessary commas have been added
to the following sentences.
  1. No commas are needed.
  2. Also included in the program will be
     speakers, awards, and music.
  3. Sue Almeda, Fran Warner, Lillian
     Rutledge, and Vanessa Grogan are in
     charge of inviting guests.
  4. Interested, enthusiastic, dedicated
     volunteers will be invited.
  5. No commas are needed.
  6. No commas are needed.
  7. On the menu will be stuffed chicken
     breasts, baked potatoes, peas, salad,
     rolls, ice cream, and coffee.
  8. The play will require the cooperation
     of talented, interested, well-rehearsed
     participants.
  9. It will include poetry, dialogue, songs,
     and music.
  10. The volunteers to be honored work
     daily, weekly, or monthly at a variety
     of tasks.

Exercise 9: Writing Sentences
with Series
page 134
Your sentences will differ from these.
Check your sentences to make sure they
are punctuated correctly.
  1. On Monday, I will have hot dogs,
     baked beans, and pickles for supper.
  2. The most interesting person I know is
     intelligent, handsome, and funny.
  3. The child laughed long, hard, and
     delightedly at the circus clowns.

Exercise 10: Correcting a Business
Letter
page 137
  1. Foster City, CA 94404
  2. Sept. 22, 1997
  3. Foster City, CA 94404
  4. Dear Dr. Green: (A colon is used in
     the greeting of a business letter.)
  5. Sincerely, (*Sincerely* is an appropriate
     closing for a business letter. A comma
     comes after it.)

Exercise 11: Chapter Review
pages 138–140
Part 1

1. An adjective describes a noun. It can tell what kind, which one, or how many.
2. An adverb describes a verb. It can tell how, when, or where.
3. Adverbs can by formed by adding *ly* to many adjectives. If the adjective ends in *y*, the *y* is changed to *i* before *ly* is added.
4. Commas are used after every item except the last one in a series of three or more items.
5. Commas are used between the city and the state in both the return address and the inside address. Commas are used between the day and the year in the date and after the closing.

You should have corrected the sentences as follows.

6. Ruth is a **happy** person. (Use an adjective to tell what kind of person Ruth is.)
7. The race car moved **quickly** around the track. (Use an adverb to tell how the car moved.)
8. Nuts, bolts, wrenches, and tools were thrown around the shop. (Use a comma after every item in a series except the last one.)
9. The men and the women agreed that life moves too rapidly. (No comma is needed with only two items.)
10. The customers **hungrily** ate the barbecued chicken. (To change *hungry* to an adverb, change the *y* to an *i* and add *ly*.)
11. The business is located in Anchorage, Alaska. (A comma is needed between the city and state.)
12. The old, battered, rusted truck limped into the station. (Use commas to separate the adjectives.)
13. The trustworthy, young, bright babysitter raised her fee.
14. The soldier looked **bravely** into the eyes of his captors. (Use an adverb to tell how the soldier looked.)
15. The date on the letter was Feb. 14, 1995. (Use a comma between the day and the year.)

Part 2

1. Add *'s*.
2. Add *'*.
3. The three endmarks are the period (.), question mark (?), and exclamation point (!).
4. c *United States* must be capitalized.
5. c *People* should not be capitalized.
6. c *They* is the subject pronoun.
7. b The verb should not end in *s* to agree with *They*.
8. c *They* is the subject pronoun.
9. c The plural subject *immigrants* needs a verb that does not end in *s*.
10. c The verb *is* is used with a singular noun.
11. a Correct as written.
12. b Commas are needed after each item in a series except the last.

CHAPTER 7

Exercise 1: Identifying Compound Subjects and Predicates
page 145

1. CS The immigrants and their host families
2. CP were happy to see each other and were eager to get acquainted
3. CS American food, clothing, and housing
4. CP was given his own bedroom and was scheduled for English lessons

Exercise 2: Compounding Subjects and Predicates
pages 145–146

Your sentences should be very similar to the following.

1. Sharon wrote a letter to her parents during lunch and mailed it on her way home.
2. Sharon and her brother planned to visit their parents for Thanksgiving.
3. They were looking forward to seeing their parents and could hardly wait to taste their mother's cooking.
4. Sharon and her brother were surprised by the answer to her letter.
5. Sharon's mother was looking forward to visiting Sharon at Thanksgiving and could hardly wait to taste Sharon's cooking!

Exercise 3: Practicing with Conjunctions and Commas
page 149

1. Thrift stores are great places to shop, and they have many bargains.
2. Some of the customers who visit them have very little money, but others just want to find a good buy.
3. Nice clothes sell quickly, so smart customers shop on the day new items are stocked.
4. Men and women go to these stores for clothes, but children like to look for toys.
5. Some shops are open at odd hours, yet shoppers fill the aisles.
6. Furniture is very inexpensive, for it has been used.
7. Many items seem in bad shape, yet they can be beautiful when repaired.

Exercise 4: Combining Sentences
pages 149–150

1. Children are fun, and many people enjoy working with them.
   OR
   Children are fun, so many people enjoy working with them.
2. Horses are farm animals, yet people keep them in cities.
   OR
   Horses are farm animals, but people keep them in cities.
3. Drugs are a serious problem, but many teenagers think they are harmless.
   OR
   Drugs are a serious problem, yet many teenagers think they are harmless.
4. Danita needed a new dress, so she went shopping this morning.
5. His team has to win this game, or Bob will lose his bet.

Exercise 5: Correcting Sentences with Connectors
pages 153–154

1. b   5. c
2. a   6. c
3. b   7. b
4. b   8. c

Exercise 6: Writing Sentences with Connectors
pages 154–155

Pay close attention to the punctuation in the answers. If you did not use the conjunction shown here, make sure your sentence makes sense.

1. The house is a mess; therefore, it must be cleaned.
2. The police searched the neighborhood for drugs; moreover, they vowed to jail all dealers.
3. After the race, the drivers were exhausted; nevertheless, they went to the party.
4. The Joneses were evicted from their apartment; furthermore, Mr. Jones lost his job.
5. Dorothy thought she would get a small raise; instead, she was surprised with a ten percent salary increase.
6. Mom asked me to get orange juice; instead, I got grape juice.
7. Electric heat is very expensive; therefore, we keep the thermostats turned down to 65 degrees.

Exercise 7: Completing Sentences with Subordinating Conjunctions
page 158

1. if, since, when, after, or because
2. After, When, Since, or Because
3. because or since
4. since or because
5. Although, Though, or After
6. If

Exercise 8: Writing Sentences with Subordinating Conjunctions
page 159

Your answers may not be exactly like these. Check to make sure your punctuation is correct and your sentences make sense.

1. When David gets home, we will show him the pictures.
2. I save money on bus fare because I ride my bike to work every day.
3. Though Chan went to the doctor yesterday, she doesn't feel any better today.
4. Before the Jellybeans recorded their first big hit in 1964, they were completely unknown.